CW01023728

Voicebot and Chatbot Design

Flexible conversational interfaces with Amazon Alexa, Google Home, and Facebook Messenger

Rachel Batish

BIRMINGHAM - MUMBAI

Voicebot and Chatbot Design

Copyright © 2018 Packt Publishing

All rights reserved. No part of this book may be reproduced, stored in a retrieval system, or transmitted in any form or by any means, without the prior written permission of the publisher, except in the case of brief quotations embedded in critical articles or reviews.

Every effort has been made in the preparation of this book to ensure the accuracy of the information presented. However, the information contained in this book is sold without warranty, either express or implied. Neither the author, nor Packt Publishing or its dealers and distributors, will be held liable for any damages caused or alleged to have been caused directly or indirectly by this book.

Packt Publishing has endeavored to provide trademark information about all of the companies and products mentioned in this book by the appropriate use of capitals. However, Packt Publishing cannot guarantee the accuracy of this information.

Acquisition Editors: Frank Pohlmann, Suresh Jain
Project Editor: Kishor Rit
Technical Editor: Saby D'silva
Proofreader: Safis Editing
Indexer: Mariammal Chettiyar
Graphics: Tom Scaria, Sandip Tadge
Production Coordinator: Sandip Tadge

First published: September 2018
Production reference: 1280918
Published by Packt Publishing Ltd.
Livery Place
35 Livery Street
Birmingham B3 2PB, UK.
ISBN 978-1-78913-962-4

www.packtpub.com

`mapt.io`

Mapt is an online digital library that gives you full access to over 5,000 books and videos, as well as industry leading tools to help you plan your personal development and advance your career. For more information, please visit our website.

Why subscribe?

- Spend less time learning and more time coding with practical eBooks and Videos from over 4,000 industry professionals
- Learn better with Skill Plans built especially for you
- Get a free eBook or video every month
- Mapt is fully searchable
- Copy and paste, print, and bookmark content

Packt.com

Did you know that Packt offers eBook versions of every book published, with PDF and ePub files available? You can upgrade to the eBook version at `www.Packt.com` and as a print book customer, you are entitled to a discount on the eBook copy. Get in touch with us at `customercare@packtpub.com` for more details.

At `www.Packt.com`, you can also read a collection of free technical articles, sign up for a range of free newsletters, and receive exclusive discounts and offers on Packt books and eBooks.

Contributors

About the author

Rachel Batish is the co-founder and CRO of Conversation.one, the build-once-deploy-everywhere platform for conversational apps, which leverages machine learning to maximize the interaction between people and devices. Rachel is responsible for the company's sales and marketing strategies, and is actively involved in the product's roadmap and in the growing voice community.

Prior to founding Conversation.one, Rachel founded Zuznow, an AI platform for building mobile apps, and led the company from $0 to $1 M in revenue.

Rachel has a BA in political science and an MA in international relations.

I would like to thank, first and foremost, my colleague and partner, Chen Levkovich, for walking with me through this fascinating journey of conversational design and for constantly challenging me to strive for more.

I would also like to dedicate this book to my beloved mother, Judith, whose voice I miss the most.

About the reviewers

Jana Bergant is a developer with 19 years, experience in full-stack web development. She has a track record of delivering web solutions. Over the last two years, her focus has shifted to online teaching and consulting. Her Udemy account alone has over 12,000 students.

Some recommendations from her students include:

"The course takes you immediately into building a chatbot using Dialogflow's functionalities. Then goes more in depth by integrating everything with a Node.js backend, which is what's really needed in real-case professional scenarios. Jana is knowledgeable but also fun and with a great energy, so following the course is easy and never boring. Strongly suggested if you want to start learning chatbot creation."

– AS

"I've learned more in a half a day than I did in a week reading through Google's documentation. Well worth the money."

– Jonnie

"Thank you for this great course. I now have my own portfolio ready in less than a week. The instructor is amazing. Looking forward to more courses from Jana."

– ST

She offers teaching and consulting to local companies and start-ups on every stage of chatbot development. Her chatbot course and Google Assistant actions development course have 12,000 students. Her plan is to publish more courses in the same field and to support her students in every aspect of chatbot development.

Sachin Bhatnagar began dabbling in computer programming and graphics at the age of 14 on a Sinclair Spectrum home computer using the BASIC language. During the early 2000s, Sachin was instrumental in crafting CRM solutions for a prominent internet service provider in India, as well as designing web-based solutions for corporations.

In 2001, Sachin ventured into computer graphics and visual effects training and production. In 2014, Sachin went back to his first love — coding, and launched a series of online training programs on the subject, and still continues to do so. His online course on chatbots is highly rated and he also consults professionally on the subject, as well as on cloud computing solutions.

From developing world class curriculum to imparting training to over five thousand students in the classroom and over twelve thousand online, Sachin has been instrumental in fueling innovation, creating brand identities, and crafting world class technology solutions for companies and individuals alike.

Packt is Searching for Authors Like You

If you're interested in becoming an author for Packt, please visit authors. packtpub.com and apply today. We have worked with thousands of developers and tech professionals, just like you, to help them share their insight with the global tech community. You can make a general application, apply for a specific hot topic that we are recruiting an author for, or submit your own idea.

TABLE OF CONTENTS

Preface

The world of conversational design opened up to me over two years ago, when my company shifted from Mobile to Voice. We were fortunate to be one of the first companies to recognize that voice is going to take over our interaction mediums, and that businesses will have to react fast to the conversational revolution that has just emerged.

And indeed, today, we can say that conversational interactions, whether through chat or voice, are changing the way we live and do business, offering an efficient, focused, and cost-effective solution that suits our needs.

However, conversational design didn't just "appear" into our lives. It is the evolution of a long human-machine communication history, in which with every step we take, we get closer and closer to naturally humanized interaction with computers.

In this book, I will highlight some of the main components of conversational design, while distinguishing between chat and voice interfaces. Although I do refer to the technicalities behind building conversational solutions, I chose to focus on the challenge of designing a successful conversational interaction that will be natural, comprehensive, and supportive of users' needs.

The world of conversational design is very dynamic and it evolves constantly. In fact, as I was writing this book, I needed to go back and update some of the chapters to keep the information up to date.

However, this is also what makes this technology so interesting and unique. We are in the midst of a revolution, and we are a main part of it, Conversational designers, developers, device-builders, and vendors are all shaping the way conversational design will be in the next decade. There is a lot to innovate, to accomplish and achieve, and as pioneers in this market, we can all make a difference and leave a mark.

Writing this book, I wanted to provide you, the readers, with an easy-to-use guide to build your first conversational applications. I've included some historical background, provided best practices on what to do and what not to do when building a chat or a voicebot, and incorporated concrete examples designed by some of the leading brands world wide.

I hope you will find this book a useful introduction to the world of conversational design and that it will inspire you to build and create new and improved experiences of human-machine interaction.

Who this book is for

This book requires a general understanding of UI building, but the coding level is kept fairly simple: a basic grasp of markup languages and JavaScript will suffice. No in-depth knowledge of Artificial Intelligence is required, except for basic concepts. Knowledge of Natural Language Processing will be helpful, but is not mandatory. Developers and product managers, and even C-level executives, will profit from this book, since it shows them the interactive, expressive side of conversational AI. It is impossible to understand modern NLP and AI products without this.

What this book covers

Chapter 1, Conversational UI is our Future, addresses the concept of conversational UIs by exploring what they are, how they evolved, their challenges, and how they will develop in the future. The chapter gives a timeline of how UI has developed over the years and the difference between voice control, chatbots, virtual assistants, and conversational solutions.

Chapter 2, How Not to Build Your Next Chat and Voicebots, discusses and analyzes the requirements for building a conversational application, by looking into *bad* examples and use cases. Sometimes, knowing what *not* to do, is more worthy than knowing what you should do.

Chapter 3, Building a Killer Conversational App, provides five tips for making a conversational application successful. Those tips are backed up by some chat and voice examples.

Chapter 4, Designing for Amazon Alexa and Google Home, takes a deep dive into the design of conversational solutions by looking at the two leading voice-enabled solutions, Amazon Alexa and Google Home. This chapter reviews both technical and voice UX recommendations and offers examples.

Chapter 5, Designing a Facebook Messenger Chatbot, discusses the structure of the Facebook Messenger platform, its advantages, and disadvantages. This chapter includes a tutorial on how to build a FB Messenger bot using its internal tools and discusses other tools that are commonly used by developers in the market.

Chapter 6, Contextual Design – Can We Make a Bot Feel More Human?, tackles the challenge of creating and building contextual conversation – one of the greatest obstacles that businesses and developers face today. In this chapter, we will learn about contextual design and provide a few recommendations on how to achieve it.

Chapter 7, Building Personalities – Your Bot Can Be a Better Human, touches on the importance of the personality of your bot, and gives guidance on how to choose it and what it should reflect when it's interacting with your clients.

Chapter 8, A View into Vertical-Specific Bots – Financial Institutions, looks at bots in the financial sector and their unique components.

Chapter 9, Travel and E-Commerce Bot – Use cases and Implementation, addresses the challenges of travel and e-commerce bots, and learning from real use cases and implementations by some leading industry players.

Chapter 10, Conversational Design Project – A Step-By-Step Guide, guides the reader through using all the concepts discussed in the book and implementing them in their first conversational application.

Chapter 11, Summary, recaps what has been discussed throughout this book and provides insights into the future of conversational design.

To get the most out of this book

To get the most out of this book, I suggest trying to gain experience with as many conversational applications as you can. Try and experiment with chatbots on various websites and on Facebook Messenger. If you have access to an Alexa device or Google Home, try to use some of the trending skills and analyze their shortfalls and successes. If you don't have either of those devices, use the Google Assistant on your mobile phone (you can download it on iPhone as well).

Download the color images

We also provide a PDF file that has color images of the screenshots/ diagrams used in this book. You can download it here: `https://www. packtpub.com/sites/default/files/downloads/9781789139624_ ColorImages.pdf`.

Conventions used

There are a number of text conventions used throughout this book.

Bold: Indicates a new term, an important word, or words that you see on the screen, for example, in menus or dialog boxes, also appear in the text like this. For example: "Select **System info** from the **Administration** panel."

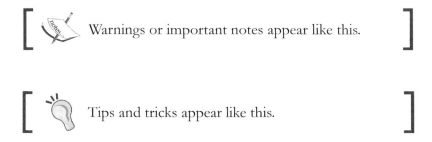

[Warnings or important notes appear like this.]

[Tips and tricks appear like this.]

Get in touch

Feedback from our readers is always welcome.

General feedback: If you have questions about any aspect of this book, mention the book title in the subject of your message and email us at `customercare@packtpub.com`.

Errata: Although we have taken every care to ensure the accuracy of our content, mistakes do happen. If you have found a mistake in this book we would be grateful if you would report this to us. Please visit, `http://www.packt.com/submit-errata`, selecting your book, clicking on the Errata Submission Form link, and entering the details.

Piracy: If you come across any illegal copies of our works in any form on the Internet, we would be grateful if you would provide us with the location address or website name. Please contact us at `copyright@packt.com` with a link to the material.

If you are interested in becoming an author: If there is a topic that you have expertise in and you are interested in either writing or contributing to a book, please visit `http://authors.packtpub.com`.

Reviews

Please leave a review. Once you have read and used this book, why not leave a review on the site that you purchased it from? Potential readers can then see and use your unbiased opinion to make purchase decisions, we at Packt can understand what you think about our products, and our authors can see your feedback on their book. Thank you!

For more information about Packt, please visit `packt.com`.

1

CONVERSATIONAL UI IS OUR FUTURE

Conversational **user interface** (**UI**) is changing the way that we interact. Intelligent assistants, **chatbots,** and voice-enabled devices, such as Amazon Alexa and Google Home, offer a new, natural, and intuitive human-machine interaction and open up a whole new world for us as humans. Chatbots and **voicebots** ease, speed up, and improve daily tasks. They increase our efficiency and, compared to humans, they are also very cost-effective for the businesses employing them.

This chapter will address the concept of conversational UIs by initially exploring what they are, how they evolved, what they offer, their challenges, and how they will develop in the future. The chapter provides an introduction to the conversational world. We will take a look at how UI has developed over the years and the difference between voice control, chatbots, virtual assistants and conversational solutions.

What is conversational UI?

Broadly speaking, conversational UI is a new form of interaction with computers that tries to mimic a "natural human conversation." To understand what this means, we can turn to the good old Oxford Dictionary and search for the definition of a conversation:

con·ver·sa·tion

/ˌkänvərˈsāSH(ə)n/ noun

A talk, especially an informal one, between two or more people, in which news and ideas are exchanged.

On Wikipedia (`https://en.wikipedia.org/wiki/Conversation`), I found some interesting additions. There, conversation is defined a little more broadly: "An interactive communication between two or more people… the development of conversational skills and etiquette is an important part of socialization."

The development of conversational skills in a new language is a frequent focus of language teaching and learning. If we sum up the two definitions, we can agree that a conversation must be:

1. Some type of communication (a talk)
2. Between more than two people
3. Interactive: ideas and thoughts must be exchanged
4. Part of a socialization process
5. Focused on learning and teaching

Now if we go back to our definition of conversational UI, we can easily identify the gaps between the classic definition of a conversation and what we define today as conversational UI.

Conversational UI, as opposed to the preceding definition:

1. Doesn't have to be oral: it could be in writing (for example, chatbots).

2. Is not just between people and is limited to two sides: in conversational UI, we have at least one form of a computer involved, and the conversation is limited to only two participants. Rarely does conversational UI involve more than two participants.

3. Is less interactive and it's hard to say whether ideas are exchanged between the two participants.

4. Is thought of as unsocialized, since we are dealing with computers and not people. However, the two main components are already there.

5. Is a medium of communication that enables natural conversation between two entities.

6. Is about learning and teaching by leveraging **Natural Language Understanding** (**NLU**), **Artificial Intelligence** (**AI**), **Machine Learning** (**ML**), and **Deep Learning** (**DL**), as computers continue to learn and develop their understanding capabilities.

The gaps that we identified above represent the future evolution of conversational UI. While it seems like there is a long way to go for us to actually be able to truly replace human-to-human interaction, with today's and future technologies, those gaps will close sooner than we think. However, let's start by taking a look at how human-computer interaction evolved over the last 50 years, before we try to predict the future.

The evolution of conversational UI

Conversational UI is part of a long evolution of human-machine interaction. The interface of this communication has evolved tremendously over the years, mostly thanks to technology improvements, but also through the imagination and vision of humans.

Science fiction books and movies predicted different forms of humanized interaction with machines for decades (some of the best-known examples are *Star Wars, 2001: A Space Odyssey*, and *Star Trek*), however, computing power was extremely scarce and expensive, so investing in this resource on UIs wasn't a high priority. Today, when our smartphones use more computing power than a supercomputer did in the past, the development of human-machine interaction is much more natural and intuitive. In this chapter, we will review the evolution of computer UI, from the textual through to the graphical and all the way to the conversational UI.

Textual interface

For many years, a textual interface was the only way to interact with computers. The textual interface used commands with a strict format and evolved into free natural language text.

Figure 1: A simple textual interaction based on commands

A good example of a common use of textual interaction is search engines. Today, if I type a sentence such as `search for a hotel in NYC` on Google or Bing (or any other search engine for that matter), the search engine will provide me with a list of relevant hotels in NYC.

Figure 2: Modern textual UI: Google's search engine

Graphical user interface (GUI)

A later evolution of human-machine interface was the **GUI**. This interface mimics the way that we perform mechanical tasks in "real life" and replaces the textual interaction.

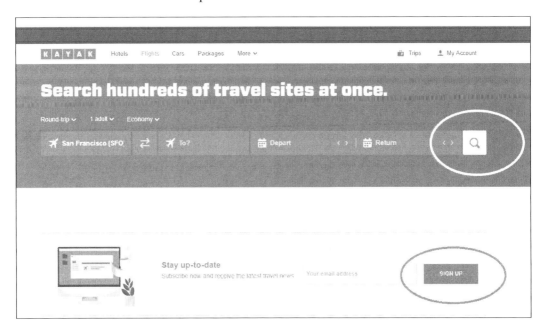

Figure 3: The GUI mimicking real-life actions

With this interface, for example, to enable/disable an action or specific capability, we will *click* a button on a screen, using a mouse (instead of writing a textual command line), mimicking a mechanical action of turning on or off a real device.

Figure 4: Microsoft Word is changing the way we interact with personal computers

The GUI became extremely popular during the 90s, with the introduction of Microsoft Windows, which became the most popular operating system for personal computers. The following evolution of GUIs came with the introduction of touchscreen devices, which eliminated the need for mediators, such as the mouse, and provided a more direct and natural way of interacting with a computer.

Figure 5: Touchscreens are eliminating the mouse

Figure 6: Touchscreens allow scrolling and clicking, mimicking manual actions

Conversational UI

The latest evolution of computer-human interaction is the conversational UI. As defined above, a conversational interaction is a new form of communication between humans and machines that includes a series of questions and answers, if not an actual exchange of thoughts.

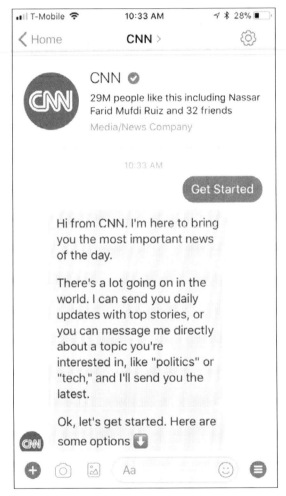

Figure 7: The CNN Facebook Messenger chatbot

In the conversational interface, we experience, once again, a form of two-sided communication, where the user asks a question and the computer will respond with an answer. In many ways, this is similar to the textual interface we introduced earlier (see the example of the search engine), however, in this case, the end user is not searching for information on the internet but is instead interacting in a one-to-one format with *someone* who delivers the answer. That *someone* is a humanized-computer entity called a *bot*.

The conversational UI mimics a text/voice interaction with a friend/service provider. Though still not a true conversation as defined in the Oxford Dictionary, it provides a free and natural experience that gets the closest to a human-human interaction that we have seen yet.

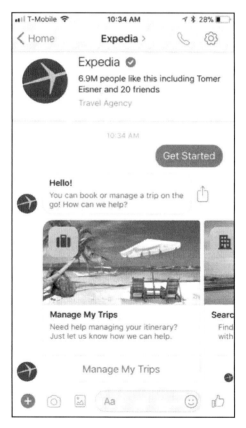

Figure 8: The Expedia Facebook Messenger chatbot

Voice-enabled conversational UI

A sub-category in the field of conversational UI is **voice-enabled conversational UI**. Whereas the shift from textual to GUI and then from GUI to conversational is defined as evolution, **conversational voice interaction** is a full paradigm shift. This new way to interact with machines, using nothing but our voice – our most basic communication and expression tool – takes human-machine relationships to a whole new level.

Computers are now capable of recognizing our voice, "understanding" our requests, responding back, and even replying with suggestions and recommendations. Being a natural interaction method for humans, voice makes it easy for young people and adults to engage with computers, in a limit-free environment.

Figure 9: Amazon Alexa and Google Home are voice-enabled devices that facilitate conversational interactions between humans and machines

The stack of conversational UI

The building blocks required to develop a modern and interactive conversational application include:

♦ Speech recognition (for voicebots)

♦ NLU

♦ Conversational level:

　○ Dictionary/samples

　○ Context

　○ Business logic

In this section, we will walk through the "journey" of a conversational interaction along the conversational stack.

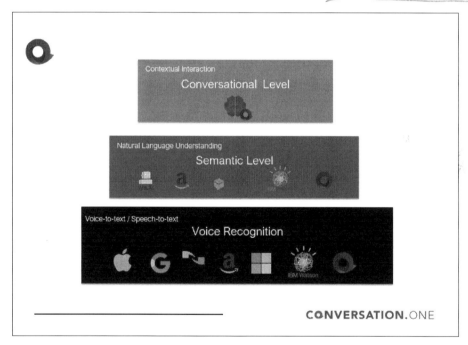

Figure 10: The conversational stack: voice recognition, NLU, and context

Voice recognition technology

Voice recognition (also known as **speech recognition** or **speech-to-text**) transcribes voice into text. The computer captures our voice with a microphone and provides a text transcription of the words. Using a simple level of text processing, we can develop a voice control feature with simple commands, such as "turn left" or "call John." Leading providers of speech recognition today include Nuance, Amazon, IBM Watson, Google, Microsoft, and Apple.

NLU

To achieve a higher level of understanding, beyond simple commands, we must include a layer of NLU. NLU fulfills the task of reading comprehension. The computer "reads the text" (in a voicebot, it will be the transcribed text from the speech recognition) and then tries to grasp the user's *intent* behind it and translate it into concrete steps.

Lets take a look at travel bot, as an example. The system identifies two individual intentions:

1. Flight booking – BookFlight

2. Hotel booking – BookHotel

When a user asks to *book a flight*, the NLU layer is what helps the bot to *understand* that the intent behind the user's request is BookFlight. However, since people don't talk like computers, and since our goal is to create a humanized experience (and not a computerized one), the NLU layer should understand or be able to connect various requests to a specific intent.

Another example is when a user says, *I need to fly to NYC*. The NLU layer is expected to understand that the user's intent is to book a flight. A more complex request for our NLU to understand would be when a user says, *I'm travelling again.*

Similarly, the NLU should connect the user's sentence to the BookFlight intent. This is a much more complex task, since the bot can't identify the word *flight* in the sentence or a destination out of a list of cities or states. Therefore, the sentence is more difficult for the bot to understand.

Computer science considers NLU to be a "hard AI problem"(*Turing Test as a Defining Feature of AI-Completeness* in *Artificial Intelligence, Evolutionary Computation and Metaheuristics (AIECM), Roman V. Yampolskiy*), meaning that even with AI (powered by deep learning) developers are still struggling to provide a high-quality solution. To call a problem AI-hard means that this problem cannot be solved by a simple specific algorithm and that means dealing with unexpected circumstances while solving any real-world problem. In NLU, those unexpected circumstances are the various configurations of words and sentences in an endless number of languages and dialects. Some leading providers of NLU are Dialogflow (previously `api.ai`, acquired by Google), `wit.ai` (acquired by Facebook), Amazon, IBM Watson, and Microsoft.

Dictionaries/samples

To build a good NLU layer that can understand people, we must provide a broad and comprehensive sample set of concepts and categories in a subject area or domain. Simply put, we need to provide a list of associated samples or, even better, a collection of possible sentences for each single intent (request) that a user can activate on our bot. If we go back to our travel example, we would need to build a comprehensive dictionary, as you can see in the following table:

User says (samples)	Related intent
I want to book my travel	BookFlight
I want to book a flight	
I need a flight	
Please book a hotel room	BookRoom
I need accommodation	

Building these dictionaries, or sets of samples, can be a tough and Sisyphean task. It is domain-specific and language-specific, and, as such, requires different configurations and tweaks from one use case to another, and from one language to another. Unlike the GUI, where the user is restricted to choosing from the web screen, the conversational UI is unique, since it offers the user an unlimited experience. However, as such, it is also very difficult to pre-configure to a level of perfection (see the AI-hard problem above). Therefore, the more samples we provide, the better the bot's NLU layer will be able to understand different requests from a user. Beware of the catch-22 in this case: the more intents we build, the more samples are required, and all those samples can easily lead to intents overlapping. For example, when a user says, *I need help*, they might mean they want to contact support, but they also might require help on how to use the app.

Context

Contextual conversation is one of the toughest challenges in conversational interaction. Being able to understand context is what makes a bot's interaction a humanized one. As mentioned previously, at its minimum, conversational UI is a series of questions and answers. However, adding a contextual aspect to it is what makes it a "true" conversational experience. By enabling context understanding, the bot can keep track of the conversation in its different stages and relate, and make a connection between, different requests. The entire flow of the conversation is taken into consideration and not just the last request.

In every conversational bot we build – either as a chatbot or a voicebot – the interaction will have two sides:

The end user will ask, *Can I book a flight?*

The bot will respond, *Yes.* The bot might also add, *Do you want to fly international?*

The end user can then approve this or respond by saying, *No, domestic.*

A contextual conversation is very different from a simple Q&A. For the preceding scenario, there were multiple different ways the user could have responded and the bot must be able to deal with all those different flows.

State machine

One methodology for dealing with different flows is to use a **state machine methodology**. This popular and simple way to describe context connects each state (phase) of the conversation to the next state, depending on the user's reaction.

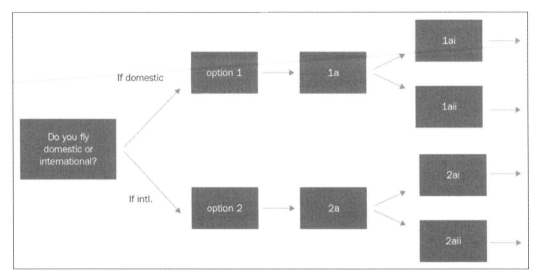

Figure 11: Building contextual conversation using a state machine
works better for simple use-cases and flows

However, the advantage of a state machine is also its disadvantage. This methodology forces us to map every possible conversational flow in advance. While it is very easy to use for building simple use cases, it is extremely difficult to understand and maintain over time, and it's impossible to use for more complicated flows (flight booking, for example, is a complex flow that can't be supported using a state machine). Another problem with the state machines method is that, even for simple use cases, to support multiple use cases with the same response, we still need to duplicate much of the work.

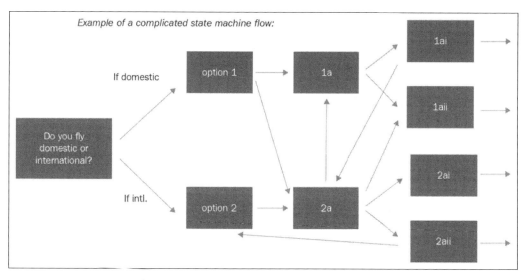

Figure 12: The disadvantage of using a state machine methodology
when building complex flows

Event-driven contextual approach

The **event-driven contextual approach** is a more suitable method for today's conversational UI. It lets the users express themselves in an unlimited flow and doesn't force them through a specific flow. Understanding that it's impossible to map the entire conversational flow in advance, the event-driven contextual approach focuses on the *context* of the user's request to gather all the information it needs in an unstructured way by minimizing all other options.

Using this methodology, the user leads the conversation and the machine analyzes the data and completes the flow at the back. This method allows us to depart from the restricting GUI state machine flow and provide human-level interaction.

In this example, the machine knows that it needs the following parameters to complete a flight:

♦ Departure location

♦ Destination

♦ Date

♦ Airline

The user in this case can fluently say, *I want to book a flight to NYC*, or *I want to fly from SF to NYC tomorrow*, or *I want to fly with Delta*.

For each of these flows, the machine will return to the user to collect the missing information:

User says	Information bot collects	Information bot requests	User replies
I want to book a flight to NYC	Destination: NYC	Departure location Date Airline	Tomorrow, from SF with Delta
I want to fly from SF to NYC tomorrow	Departure: SF Destination: NY Date: Tomorrow	Airline	With Delta
I want to fly with Delta to NYC	Destination: NYC Airline: Delta	Departure location Date	From NY, tomorrow

By building a conversational flow in an event-driven contextual approach, we succeed in mimicking our interaction with a human agent. When booking a flight with a travel agent, I start the conversation and provide the details that I know. The agent, in return, will ask me only for the missing details and won't force me to state each detail at a certain time.

Business logic/dynamic data

At this stage, I think we can agree that building a conversational UI is not an easy task. In fact, many bots today don't use NLU and avoid free-speech interaction. We had great expectations of chatbots and with those high expectations came a great disappointment. This is why many chatbots and voicebots today provide mostly simple Q&A flows.

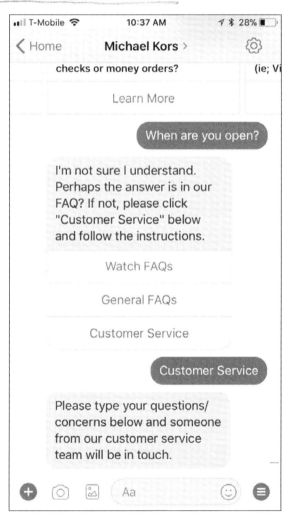

Figure 13: The Michael Kors Facebook Messenger bot: conversational UI minimized to a simple Q&A flow with no contextuality

Most of those bots have a limited offering and the business logic is connected to two-to-three specific use cases, such as opening hours or a phone number, no matter what the user is asking for. In other very popular chat interfaces, bots are still leaning on the GUI, offering a menu selection and eliminating free text.

Figure 14: The Michael Kors Facebook Messenger bot:
forcing graphic UI on conversational UI mediums

However, if we are building a true conversational communication between our bot and our users, we must make sure that we connect it to a dynamic business logic. So, after we have enabled speech recognition, worked on our NLU, built samples, and developed an event-driven contextual flow, it is time to connect our bot to dynamic data. To reach real-time data, and to be able to run transactions, our bot needs to connect to the business logic of our application. This can be done through the usage of APIs to your backend systems.

Going back to our flight booking bot, we would need to retrieve real-time data on when the next flight from SF to NYC is, what seats are still available, and what the price is for the flight. Our APIs can also help us to complete the order and approve a payment. If you are lacking APIs for some of the needed data and functions, you can develop new ones or use screen-scraping techniques to avoid a complex development.

Challenges and gaps in conversational UI

Conversational UI is still new to us and, as such, there are still challenges and gaps that prevent it from reaching its full potential. Technology has improved greatly over the years to get us to where we are, but, although we are far from *HAL 9000* (from the movie *2001: A Space Odyssey*, in which a computer program interacts freely with the ship's astronaut crew and controls the systems of the Discovery One spacecraft using *thinking* and *feeling*), we must keep in mind that even HAL had some malfunctions. In this section, I will list the five main challenges that technology and bot designers will have to address in the next few years.

NLU is an AI-hard problem

As human-machine interaction becomes more sophisticated, natural, and humanized, the harder it is to build and develop it. While creating a simple command-line text-based interface can be done by any developer, a high-quality UI in the form of a chatbot or voicebot requires many experts, including chat and voice designers and NLU specialists, both of which are very hard to find.

Natural language understanding is the attempt to mimic reading comprehension by a machine. It is a subtopic of AI and, as mentioned earlier, it is an **AI-hard** (or **AI-complete**) problem. An AI-hard problem is equivalent to solving the central AI problem: making computers as intelligent as people (`https://en.wikipedia.org/wiki/AI-complete`). Why is it so difficult? As discussed above, when responding to a conversational UI, there is an infinite number of unknown and unexpected features in the input, within an infinite number of options of syntactic and semantic schemes to apply to it. This means that when we chat or talk to a bot, just as when we talk to another person, we are unlimited in what we can say. We are not restricted to keeping to a specific GUI path: we are free to ask about anything and everything.

One way to tackle the NLU AI-hard issue is to focus and limit the computer's understanding to a specific theme, subject, or use case. When I go to the doctor, I'm probably not going to consult with him about the return I will yield when investing in the NY stock exchange. When I visit the doctor, I am within a *specific context*: I don't feel well, I need a new subscription to a medication, and so on. In fact, just within a doctor scenario, there are so many use cases that we will have to predefine, so it would make sense to break those down into sub-use cases, to help improve our NLU in sub-domain contexts (pediatrician, gynecology, oncology, and so on).

If we go back to our travel example, we can train the NLU layer of our bot to be able to respond to everything related to the booking of flights. In this case, we mimic a possible conversation between the user and a travel agent. While a human travel agent can help us with additional tasks, such as finding a hotel, planning our trip, and more, in this use case we will stay within the context of booking flights to maximize the experience and the responses.

Accuracy level

A major derivative of the NLU problem is the accuracy level of the conversation. Even when limiting our bot to a specific use case, the need to cover all possible requests, in each form of language, makes it very hard to create a good **user experience (UX)**. In fact, more than 70% of the interactions we have with machines fail (https://www.fool.com/investing/2017/02/28/facebook-incs-chatbots-hit-a-70-failure-rate.aspx). While users are willing to try and address their needs quickly with an automated system, they are unforgiving once the system fails to serve them.

The accuracy of the level of understanding is dependent on the number of preconfigured *samples* in the bot. Those samples are sentences that users say that represent their request or intent. The bot, thereafter, translates them into actions. For every request, there are hundreds of such sentences. For complex requests, where there are also many parameters involved (such as our flight booking bot example), there are thousands, if not tens of thousands of them. This remains an unsolved problem today and, as a result, many bots today offer a poor experience to their users, which stays within very limited boundaries.

From GUI to CUI and VUI

The transition from GUI to **conversational UI** (**CUI**), as well as to **conversational user experience** (**CUX**), and **voice user experience** (**VUX**) introduces many challenges within this paradigm shift that we are witnessing. Beyond the unlimited options that we discussed above, as part of the AI-hard problem raised around NLU, when building a conversational UI, and especially a voice UI and UX, there is a challenge of exposing the user to your offer in a *screenless* environment.

When I go to the store, I can see all the items I can choose from and purchase, and I can ask the salesperson for more help. A good salesperson will help me and recommend items that they think I should be made aware of in the store. When I shop online, I can view all the items that are available for me to purchase and can also search for something specific and browse through the various results. Here, as well, I can get recommendations, sometimes based on my previous purchases, in different graphical forms such as pop-ups or newsletters. Exposing the user to your offering within a text or a voice conversational UI is extremely difficult. Just as a conversational UI is limited in nature (focusing on specific use cases, within a certain context), the ways to expose the user to what you offer, or how you can help him/her, are limited as well.

Chatbots

Many chatbots offer a menu-based interaction, providing options to choose from. This way, the conversation is limited to a specific flow (state machine supported), but the added value is that the user can be exposed to additional information. The problem with this solution is that it inherits the GUI experience into the CUI and very often offers very little value.

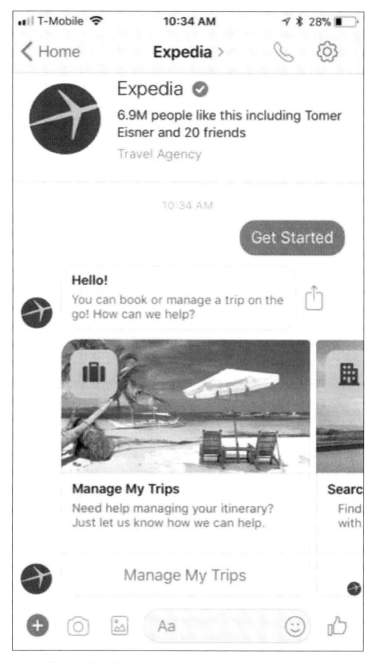

Figure 15: The Expedia Facebook Messenger bot:
is a menu-based interaction conversational?

Voicebots

In the case of voicebots, we often witness a "help" section, which provides the user with a list of actions they can perform when talking to the bot. This will be in the form of an introduction to the application, offering a few examples of what the user can ask. Going back to our flight example, imagine that a user says, *Ok Google, open travel bot*. The first response can be *Welcome to Travel Bot! How can I help you? You can ask me: what is the next flight to NYC from SF?* In addition, voice-enabled devices, such as Amazon Alexa and Google Home, provide users with an instruction cart that gives some examples of questions. The companies also send out a weekly newsletter with new capabilities.

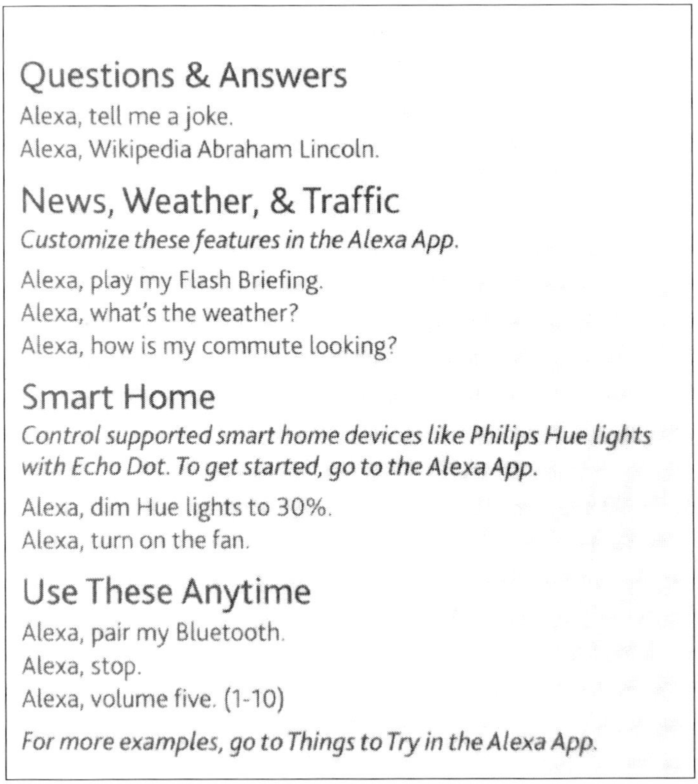

Questions & Answers
Alexa, tell me a joke.
Alexa, Wikipedia Abraham Lincoln.

News, Weather, & Traffic
Customize these features in the Alexa App.

Alexa, play my Flash Briefing.
Alexa, what's the weather?
Alexa, how is my commute looking?

Smart Home
Control supported smart home devices like Philips Hue lights with Echo Dot. To get started, go to the Alexa App.

Alexa, dim Hue lights to 30%.
Alexa, turn on the fan.

Use These Anytime
Alexa, pair my Bluetooth.
Alexa, stop.
Alexa, volume five. (1-10)

For more examples, go to Things to Try in the Alexa App.

Figure 16: The Amazon Echo jump-start cart for first-time users, which exposes users to basic capabilities

Non-implicit contextual conversation

I mentioned a couple of times the need to build contextual conversational UI and UX, and I will dedicate a full chapter (*Chapter 3, Building a Killer Conversational App*) to this in the book. Being a major challenge in today's conversational UI development, I believe that it deserves one more mention in this section.

We expect bots to replace humans – not computers. The conversational UI mimics my interaction with a human, whether through text or voice. Even when we limit the interaction to a specific use case and include all possible sample sentences that could prompt a question, there is one thing that is very difficult to predict within a contextual conversation: *non-implicit* requests.

If I call my travel agent and excitedly tell her that my daughter's 6th birthday is coming up, she might "do the math" and understand that we are planning a family trip to Disneyland. She will then extract all the parameters needed to complete my request:

1. Dates
2. Number of people/adults/kids
3. Flights
4. Hotels for the dates
5. Car rental
6. Allergies and more…

Even though I haven't *explicitly* requested her help to plan a trip to Disneyland, the travel agent will be able to connect the dots and respond to my request. Training a machine to do that, that is, to react to non-implicit requests, remains a huge challenge in today's technology stack. However, the good news is that AI technologies and, more specifically, machine learning and deep learning, will become very useful in the next couple of years for tackling this challenge.

Security and privacy

One very controversial aspect when discussing chatbots and voicebots is security and, more specifically, the privacy around it. In today's world, chatbot and voicebot platforms are controlled by some of the leading corporations and our data and information become their assets. Although Google, Amazon, and Facebook have been collecting private data for quite a while (whenever we searched the web, purchased items on Amazon, or just posted something on Facebook), now those companies "listen" to us outside of the web/app environment: they are in our homes and in every private message. Recently, Amazon Alexa was accused of recording a private conversation of a man at his home and sending it to his boss, without that person's consent.

The "constantly listening" functionality reminds many of George Orwell's *1984* and the party-monitoring telescreen that was designed to simultaneously broadcast entertainment and listen in to people's conversations to detect disorders. Although Orwell's telescreen was used by a tyranny to control its people, whereas today's solutions are owned by commercial corporations, one cannot help but wonder what the implications of using such devices will be in the future.

Conversational channels controlled by the above corporations have also become a challenge for businesses that are forced into running their customers' interactions through third-party channels. Where five years ago businesses were reluctant about shifting their data centers to the cloud, today it has no meaning at all, when data is being transferred through additional channels anyway.

This is important for us to understand when we design our chatbots and voicebots. Mainly, we should protect our customers' data and, where needed, obey the relevant country's/state's regulations. We should make sure we are not asking for specific data, such as SSN or credit card numbers and, for the time being, use complementary ways to get that, such as rerouting the user to a secure site to complete registration.

Summary

Intelligent assistance, chatbots, voicebots, and voice-enabled devices, such as Amazon Echo and Google Home, have stormed into our lives, offering many ways to improve daily tasks, through natural human-computer communication. In fact, some of the applications that we use today already take advantage of voice/chat-enabled interaction to ease our lives. Whether we are turning the lights on and off in our living room with a simple voice command or shopping online with a Facebook Messenger bot, conversational UI makes our interactions more focused and efficient.

Fast-forward from today, we can assume that conversational UI, and more specifically voice-enabled communication, will replace all interactions with computers. In the movie *Her* (2013), written and directed by Spike Jonze, an unseen computer bot communicates with the main character using voice. This voicebot (played by Scarlett Johansson) assists, guides, and consults the main character on any possible matter. It is a personal assistant on steroids.

Its knowledge is unlimited, it continues to learn all the time, it can create a conversation (a true exchange of ideas), and at the end it can even understand feelings (however, it still doesn't feel itself). However, as we've seen above, with current technology, real-life conversational UI still lacks many of the components seen in *Her* and faces unsolved challenges and question marks around it. The experience is limited for the user, as it's still mostly un-contextual and bots are far from understanding feelings or social situations.

Nevertheless, with all the limitations we experience today, creating a supercomputer that knows everything is more within reach than creating a super-knowledgeable person. Technology, whether in the form of advanced AI, ML, or DL methodologies, will solve most of those challenges and make the progress needed to build successful bot assistants.

What might take a bit more time to transform is human skepticism: conversational UI is also limited because its users are still very skeptical of it. Aware of its limitations, we stick to what works best and tend to not challenge it too much. When comparing children-bot interaction with that of adults, it is clear to see that while the latter group stays within specific boundaries of usage, the former interacts with the bots as they are real adult humans – knowledgeable about almost everything. It might be a classic chicken or the egg dilemma, but one thing is for sure: the journey has started and there's no going back.

References

- ◆ https://en.wikipedia.org/wiki/Conversation

- ◆ *Turing Test as a Defining Feature of AI-Completeness* in *Artificial Intelligence, Evolutionary Computation and Metaheuristics (AIECM), Roman V. Yampolskiy*

- ◆ https://en.wikipedia.org/wiki/AI-complete

- ◆ https://www.fool.com/investing/2017/02/28/facebook-incs-chatbots-hit-a-70-failure-rate.aspdx

2

How Not to Build Your Next Chat and Voicebots

In the previous chapter, we talked at length about the evolution of UI and, more specifically, conversational UI. We discussed the technical stacks of conversational solutions, as well as the differences between voice and chat solutions. We focused on some of the challenges of evolving those solutions and explored some ideas on how to do this.

The next few chapters will provide tips and ideas on how to build a successful conversational UI for both chat and voice applications. However, before we start analyzing the requirements for a conversational application, I would like to give some thought to conversational UI and how building it wrongly can make it bad.

Why are we building a conversational UI?

Why do we need conversational UI? What was lacking in our GUI with computers that required the development of a new UI in our lives? We mentioned in the previous chapter that conversational UI allows us to interact in quick Q&A sessions with computers, by mimicking a text or voice interaction with a friend or service provider.

In both chat and voice interaction, the goal is, once again, to make our lives easy (or at least easier than they are already). It starts with simple home capabilities, such as turning on and off the lights by talking to a device, and it can go all the way to booking flights as we drive our car, without lifting a finger. Since chat and voice are still commonly used differently, I will refer to the purpose of each separately in the following sub-sections.

Chats and chatbots

Text has become a primary interaction method between people. About 50% of adults aged 18-24 say text conversations are just as meaningful as a phone call and 90% of teens with cell phones actively text (http://www.pewinternet.org/2015/04/09/teens-social-media-technology-2015/). A text message is short, focused, and cuts to the chase. It's faster than making a phone call and the response rate is higher as well (https://www.textrequest.com/blog/texting-statistics-answer-questions/). We don't call service providers so often anymore, but we do visit their website. The website offers many options for us as users, but just like phone calls, information is not focused: it's all over the place and it may take us some time to find what we are looking for.

The first method for solving this problem was chat solutions, which involved a real agent on the other side. This option offered the convenience of a text conversation, as if we were talking to a friend. Talking to a chat function on a website allows us to ask that one specific question that we have, without needing to browse for hours for the information we are looking for. Indeed, chat platforms skyrocketed. However, whereas websites gave businesses a way to reduce the burden on customer support, by offering everything online, chat solutions increased that burden again, demanding more agents to serve people looking for focused and fast answers on their website or app.

With companies dealing once again with issues of costs and scalability, an automated solution was needed. If the current popular interaction method for us as humans is chat, then it only makes sense that our automated interaction methods mimic this as well. The purpose of chatbots is to enable a scalable and cost-effective solution for businesses to automate their customer-oriented interactions. The user could be a customer or an employee within a company who requires internal support.

Taking on the assumption that many of the requests coming from users are repeatable, the goal is to create a chatbot that can at least provide answers to as many questions as possible automatically and then transfer the customer to a human agent when the automatic interaction fails.

Voicebots, IVAs, and voice-enabled interaction

Voice activation is not new. We have all experienced automatic phone systems (known also as **IVR**s or **Voice Response Systems**) where we are required to click an extension number – or say the number – however, this is far from being a conversational communication (based on what we defined in *Chapter 1, Conversational UI is our Future*).

Voice-enabled devices, such as Amazon Echo and Google Home, started by offering specific home commands and capabilities. To ease our lives, we don't have to turn on and off the lights in our living room; we can just ask Alexa to do so and the task will be taken care of. The same can be done if we forgot to close our garage door or turn on the heater. Many of those functionalities could have already been achieved using dedicated mobile apps. However, the voice element was a game changer. We are not required to stop our life in order to activate our phones; we can just *say* it and it happens. Just like magic!

Moving from *voice-human* interaction, we shifted to *text communication* and then again to *voice*. However, this time our interaction is kept short and focused. We use our voice to express what we want, but we don't *need* to talk to another person to achieve it. Voice-enabled conversations provide us with the best of both worlds!

What your bot shouldn't be

Now that we know the purpose of chatbots and voicebots, it can help us to understand the fundamentals of one of the most common mistakes made by chat designers and developers, which eventually leads to all other mistakes: developing conversational UI based on their application's GUI.

A bot's experience *should not* imitate your web/app experience; it should mimic your agent, which is your service provider – a human!

Rather than leveraging voice and conversational capabilities by replicating real-world interactions, many bot developers and designers try to imitate the behavior of previous human-computer UIs and, more specifically, those of digital channels, such as websites/mobile apps. Instead of building a voice UX that reflects the conversations we generally have with our banker or our travel agent, developers force conversational UIs to imitate bank mobile apps or websites.

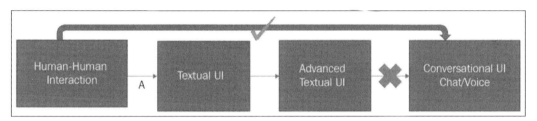

Figure 1: Don't replicate the web experience

A successful conversational UI will bring the human to the bot. Try to think what your phone call/store interaction would be like with a human and bring it to life in your chat/voice application.

Define your use cases – not too little and not too much

Many businesses struggle to identify the use cases where a bot can replace a human interaction. This is usually a result of the relatively poor experiences that today's bots provide.

Poor automated experience is a consequence of either:

♦ The "too little" scenario, where a bot offers very little and therefore has no value for the end user

♦ The "too much" scenario, where a bot sets high hopes for what it can do, but then fails to meet those expectations

In both cases, the bot is unsuccessful in fulfilling its purpose. Due to technology limitations, or bad design, it has failed to offer a fast and scalable service to the customer and failed to reduce the business' costs. Finding the **minimum viable product (MVP)** is crucial for the success of any chat/voice application, but be aware of "burning" users by offering a limited product that does not provide value. You can start with simpler types of features, but then you should develop a second level of features that provides the user with a richer experience. By offering a full-service application, you make sure that users continue to use the conversational application and don't fall back to the website, the mobile app, or the call center, or, even worse, you lose them.

As presented in the previous chapter, building a conversational design is a challenging task. While trying to simplify it, bot-development frameworks offer an easy and intuitive platform to build chatbots, with no development skills needed. In some cases, those bots have no NLU capabilities and are very limited in the understanding level of an interaction. In such cases, the user will have to ask a specific question in a certain way to get a response. If the user fails to ask the question as was preconfigured, the bot will not be able to provide the user with an answer. Understanding that this can be very limiting, some bot-development frameworks took on the menu-based structure, which eliminates the user's conversational interactions and simply offers a selection of capabilities that the user can choose from.

In such cases, the user is led in the conversation and can't ask for anything that isn't on the menu. This is clearly the most obvious form of transition that bot developers are making from GUI to CUI.

In the following example, the bot didn't understand my request, even though I selected it from the menu. After the "speak to an advisor" button was offered to me, I wrote that *I want to talk with someone*. However, the bot didn't understand my request:

Figure 2: A failed interaction with the EatOut Facebook Messenger chatbot

I then tried to use the exact same wording to ask for "Cuisines," but once again the system failed to understand my request:

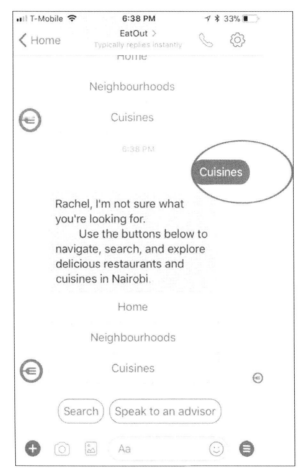

Figure 3: A failed exact-matching request using
the EatOut Facebook Messenger bot

On the Expedia chatbot, the experience was better. I wrote, *I'm looking for hotel.* The system was quick to understand me and continued the conversation, asking me in what city:

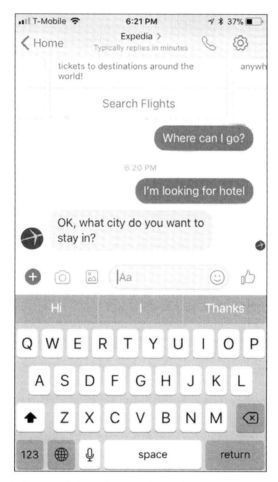

Figure 4: Successful understanding of the Expedia Facebook Messenger bot with a contextual sequence

However, I got a different result with this wording: *I need a place to sleep.*

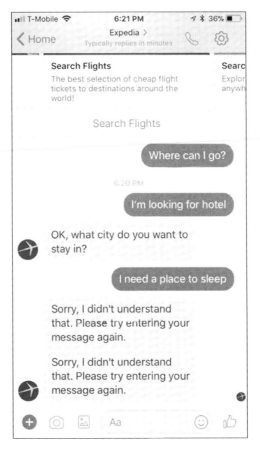

Figure 5: Lack of samples of sentences makes it hard for the NLU to understand a request in the Expedia Facebook Messenger bot

The system didn't understand my "intent" and asked me to rephrase my request.

To sum it up, the preceding examples demonstrate why use cases that are offered on various chatbots are somehow limited and in many cases also not very valuable. The information offered on these bots can be easily found on the website/app, so it can be a good start, but it symbolizes the too little functionality that continues to disappoint.

On the other hand, although we envision a "know-it-all intelligent assistant" in our future, for now, a bot that doesn't limit the user to some extent will also fail very quickly. There must be a balance between the amount of use cases and the number of supported samples. It's a width and depth challenge. The user should be informed what they can ask and what the automated solution can offer him/her and then, when the system fails, it can transfer the conversation to a real human.

In the Expedia example, we were limited to a certain scope and this is perfectly fine because, after all, even a human agent can't answer everything. However, what this chatbot failed to do was to allow us to *interact freely within the scope of the offering*, failing to understand our intent the moment we chose a different set of words.

Don't just build and forget

Conversational UI is a relatively new trend and it is also extremely dynamic. Whether supporting new types of devices and channels, adding new functionalities, or improving the UI and UX, the first version of chat and voice applications is just the beginning.

Learn from the client experience, track where your solution fails, and measure whether it offers any value at all to your clients. It is a continuous evolution. Remember, the greatest challenge of conversational UI is in many cases less the technical constraints and more the linguistic ones. Most importantly, allow your users to interact freely within a specific limited space, but also to expand the space that is automatically supported. If you start by offering five functionalities, see how you can expand that and offer more with each version you release.

Summary

In this chapter, we discussed some of the most common mistakes in voice and chat applications. In some cases, those mistakes have evolved over time through how conversational applications are developed and used, and some of those mistakes are based on a lack of knowledge (and thinking) and can be easily avoided. Although chat and voice applications are not yet the all-knowing personal assistant we want them to be, there are three main components that can be easily achieved to improve the experience and success of those apps.

Keeping in mind that the goal of both chat and voice interactions is to make our lives easy can help us to solve many of today's chat and voice challenges. Use chatbots and voicebots to solve problems that are repeatable, but make sure not to drive your users crazy, as they struggle to figure out how to use them. With this in mind, I'm summarizing our three "don'ts":

1. Don't imitate your web functionality! Your chatbots and voicebots are replacing human functionality, not the GUI, so build them that way!

2. Don't provide too little, but don't try to cover too much: don't build a bot just for the purpose of having a bot. Try to understand the value the bot brings to your clients and how it serves you, for example, reducing an agent's workload, generating leads, or providing better service at scale.

3. Keep it growing. Like all other digital products, voicebots and chatbots are growing solutions. They evolve in their coverage, as well as functionality; they change and grow as technology improves and they can become smarter! The more they grow, the better they become!

In the next chapter, we will provide recommendations on how to successfully build your conversational application. Now that we know what we shouldn't do, it's time to learn what we should do!

References

♦ `http://www.pewinternet.org/2015/04/09/teens-social-media-technology-2015/`

♦ See additional statistics on texting here: `https://www.textrequest.com/blog/texting-statistics-answer-questions/`

～ 3 ～

Building a Killer Conversational App

By now, we all agree that CUI is changing the way that we interact with our devices. We also understand that virtual assistants, chatbots, and voice-controlled devices offer a new, natural, and intuitive human-machine interaction, opening up a whole new commercial world for us. While CUI is still a new field in computing and an extremely dynamic one, we can already find a few success stories.

In this chapter, I will provide five tips for making a conversational application successful, which will help you to build your own killer conversational application. I will also offer chat and voice examples as support.

Find the direct path to initial success

Voice control and CUI are not that new. There were a few attempts in the past to make them possible and even the good old Nokia feature phones had voice control capabilities. However, since the technology was still immature, most of those trials didn't succeed. With zero patience for failure, after one or two unsuccessful tries, users just moved on or fell back to the web or mobile apps.

Interactive voice response (IVR) systems are also a good example of a voice-controlled solution and a promising idea with a really bad implementation. In fact, more than 80% of IVR users say they hate the experience (https://www.nice.com/engage/blog/Everybody-Hates-IVR-2183). So how do we find the direct path to success?

#1

Help your users to ask the right questions.

Although this sounds obvious, it is actually crucial to the success of your chatbot or voicebot. I learned that when I initially set up my Amazon Echo device at home. Using a complementary mobile app, I was directed to ask Alexa specific questions, to which she had good answers to, such as *Alexa, what is the time?* or *Alexa, what is the weather today?* I immediately received correct answers and therefore wasn't discouraged by a default response saying, *Sorry, I don't have an answer to that question.*

By providing the user with a successful experience, we encourage them to trust the system and to understand that, although it has its limitations, it is really good in some specific areas. As time passes, different devices continue to evolve and continue to expand their support and capabilities, both internally and by leveraging third parties. To help users to discover new functions, some solutions, such as Amazon Alexa and Google Home, send a weekly newsletter with the highlights of their latest capabilities. In the following email, Amazon Alexa is literally providing a list of questions that I should ask Alexa in my next interaction with it, and it also exposes me to new functionalities such as making a donation.

amazonecho

I believe the best ships are friend ships. Let's row.
Just ask, "Alexa, tell me a friendship story."

THINGS TO TRY

- "Alexa, what's the news?"
- "Alexa, make a donation."
  Alexa and Amazon Pay make it easy to donate by just using your
  voice. Learn more.
- "Alexa, why is Pluto not a planet?"
- "Alexa, translate 'good morning' in Japanese."
- "Alexa, open TuneIn Live."
  Listen to home and away games for your favorite sports teams with a
  free trial of the TuneIn Live skill. Learn more.
- "Alexa, what's your favorite word?"
- "Alexa, who's leading the Masters?"
- "Alexa, play 'Your Song' by Lady Gaga."
  Celebrate Elton John's music with Coldplay, Lady Gaga, and many
  more, as they reimagine some of his biggest hits. Learn more.
- "Alexa, set a sleep timer for ten minutes."
  When playing music, you can ask Alexa to set a sleep timer so that
  your music will automatically shut off.
- "Alexa, who is your favorite poet?"
- "Alexa, tell me a baseball joke."
- "Alexa, read my audiobook."
- "Alexa, teach me something."
- "Alexa, why is water wet?"
- "Alexa, how do I set up calling and messaging?"
- "Alexa, give me a tongue twister."

MOST REQUESTED

- **Video game**: "Alexa, what is Fortnite Battle Royale?"
- **Storytime skill**: "Alexa, open Amazon Storytime."
- **Store hours**: "Alexa, what time does Costco open?"

Figure 1: From the Amazon Alexa weekly emails "What's new with Alexa?"

On Google Home/Assistant, Google has chosen topics that it recommends its users to interact with. Here as well, the end user is exposed to new offerings/capabilities/knowledge bases, which may give them the trust needed to ask similar questions on other topics.

Figure 2: From the Google Home newsletter

Other chat and voice providers can take advantage of this email communication idea to encourage their users to further interact with their chatbots or voicebots and expose them to new capabilities. The simplest way of encouraging usage is adding a dynamic "welcoming" message to chat and voice applications, which includes new features that have been enabled. Capital One, for example, updates this information every now and then, exposing its users to new functionalities. On Alexa, it sounds like this: *Welcome to Capital One. You can ask me for things like account balance and recent transactions.*

Another way to do this – especially if you are reaching out to a random group of people – is to initiate discovery during an interaction with the user (I call this contextual discovery). For example, a banking chatbot offers information on account balances. Imagine that the user asks, *What's my account balance?*

The system gives its response: *Your checking account balance is $5,000 USD.* The bank has recently activated the option to transfer money between accounts. To expose this information to its users, it leverages the bot to prompt a rational suggestion to the user and say, *Did you know you can now transfer money between accounts? Would you like me to transfer $1,000 to your savings account?*

As you can see, the discovery process was done in context with the user's actions. Not only does the user know that he/she can now transfer money between two accounts, but they can also experience it immediately, within the relevant context.

To sum up tip #1, by finding the direct path to initial success, your users will be encouraged to further explore and discover your automated solutions and will not fall back to other channels. The challenge is, of course, to continuously expose users to new functionalities, made available on your chatbots and voicebots, preferably in a contextual manner.

Think like a search engine, not a command line

We already discussed the evolution of conversational UIs and their connection to the command line and search engines. The user is required to provide the computer with a textual question and in return they get a textual response. However, there is one great differentiator between the user experience of command line versus a search engine. Whereas in a command line the user will receive an error message if they don't use the exact correct format, search engines always return a result, whether it's the answer to your question, something close enough to your question, or even a suggestion for a different search.

In the following example, I asked Google for information about conversational applications, however, I made a mistake in my spelling. Google didn't reply with an *error message,* but rather tried to fix my request and suggested a possible reply (it does let me know that there are no results for my search).

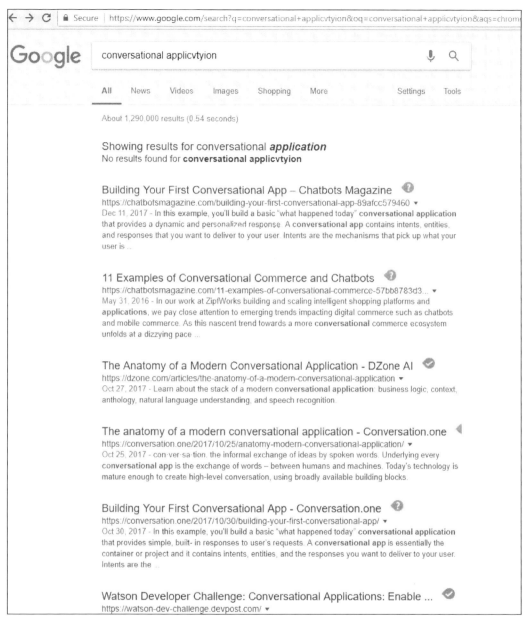

Figure 3: Think like a search engine: try to understand
what your user's intention was (Google search)

The same is true for chatbots and voicebots. Whether the user made a spelling mistake or even used a different wording for an existing request, it doesn't mean the system should prompt an error message. On the contrary, the system should make the effort to provide the closest relevant response or offer a correction. For example, to play music with Google Home a user can say, *Hey Google, please play the Ed Sheeran station from Pandora.* Google will reach out to their Pandora account and search for Ed Sheeran songs to play. In this case, the user is very explicit. However, the user can also use a shorter version of his/her request and simply say, *Hey Google, please play Ed Sheeran songs.* In this interaction, Google will decide on the enabled *music service* and search for an Ed Sheeran station to play from. In cases where the user is the least explicit and simply says, *Hey Google, play music,* Google will search for the user's enabled music service and play one of their suggested favorite stations.

Acting like a search engine opens up a vast variety of options for businesses and their bots to reply to their users and even surprise them. This idea of acting like a search engine brings our discussion back to the necessity of incorporating an NLU engine in your chat/voicebots. Depending on the NLU you choose, you could generate much more value for your users, based on the understanding level of the bot. The higher the accuracy level is, the more your chatbot can act as a search engine and the less it will act as a command line.

Many Facebook Messenger bots don't even let the user express their needs and instead automatically offer a list of options that guides them through the process of receiving customer support.

In some cases, there isn't even a textbox to write inside (see the following Spotify example). While I had a nice onboarding experience, and I was guided through the process, I wasn't free to enter my requests: I could only choose from a predefined list.

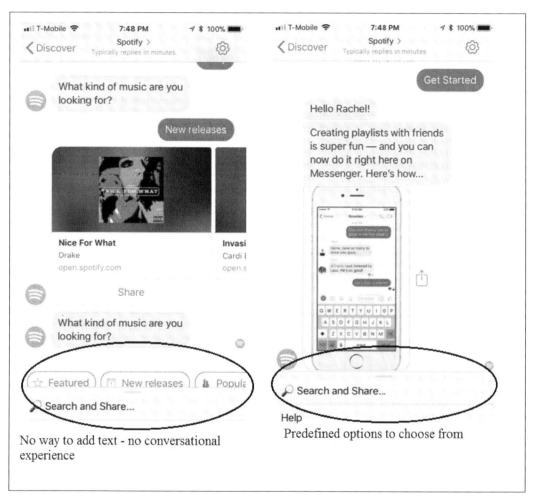

Figure 4: Keeping it conversational means letting your users express themselves freely (Spotify FB bot).

On the following Western Union chatbot example, I have the option of texting with the chatbot, but no matter what I ask, I'm referred to the menu. On one hand, I'm still getting an error message to a question that I asked, which obviously means that the bot does not provide a solution. On the other hand, the bot still tries to prompt me with discovery options that are relevant for my choice.

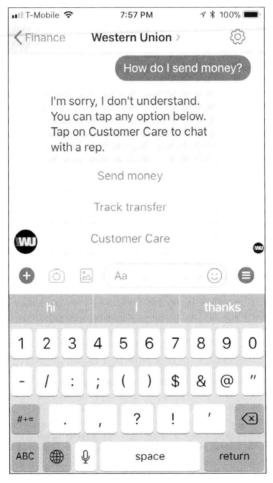

Figure 5: Failure in understanding supported options (Western Union FB bot)

In this last example, I chose Domino's pizza. Domino's pizza is one of the most advanced companies when it comes to digital solutions and is a great reference in most cases. In this example, for some reason, I couldn't order a garlic bread (although it appears in the bot's discovery on the picture). I would have expected the bot to tell me that it's impossible to order garlic bread at the moment, or at least try to understand what I was asking for or suggest other suitable options.

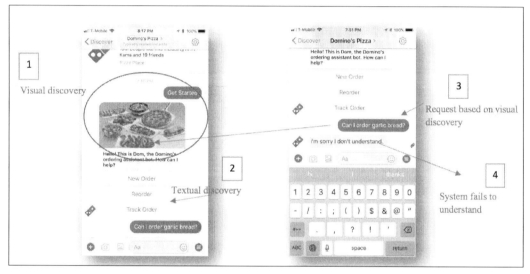

Figure 6: Promote what you have and don't fail the user (Domino's Pizza FB bot)

To sum up tip #2, user experience is the most crucial factor for the success (or failure) of an automated interaction. Combining it with tip #1, keep in mind that your role is to help your users to get what they are asking for. It's not their role to figure out bots; it's your role to figure out what's the best way to deliver the best results.

Give your bot a "personality," but don't pretend it's a human

We dedicate *Chapter 7, Building Personalities – Your Bot can be a Better Human*, to building personalities into an automated solution, but I believe this topic must be included in our list of tips. Your bot, just like any digital solution you provide today, should have a personality that makes sense for your brand. It can be visual, but it can also be enabled over voice. Whether it is a character you use for your brand or something created for your bot, personality is more than just the bot's icon. It's the language that it "speaks," the type of interaction that it has, and the environment it creates. In any case, don't try to pretend that your bot is a human talking with your clients. People tend to ask bots questions like *are you a bot?*, and sometimes even try to make them fail by asking questions that are not related to the conversation (like asking how much *30*4,000* is or what the bot thinks of "a specific event"). Let your users know that it's a bot that they are talking to and that it's there to help. This way, the user has no incentive to intentionally trip up the bot.

Chatbot examples

The following are a few examples of chatbots with matching personalities.

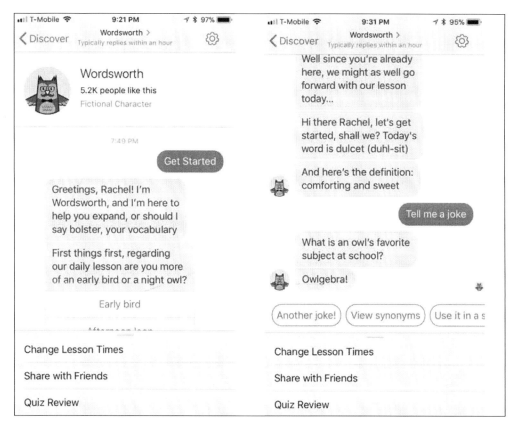

Figure 7: Expand your vocabulary with a word a day (Wordsworth)

The Wordsworth bot has the personality of an owl. Owl symbolizes wisdom, which fits very well with the purpose of the bot: to enrich the user's vocabulary. However, we can see that this bot has more than just an owl as its "presenter": pay attention to the language and word games, and even the joke at the end. Jokes are a great way to deliver personality.

From those two screenshots only, we can easily capture a specific image of this bot, what it represents, and what it's here to do.

The DIY-Crafts-HandMade bot has a different personality, which signals something light and fun. The language used is much more conversational (and less didactic) and there's a lot of usage of icons and emojis. It's clear that this bot was created for girls/women and offers the end user a close "friend" to help them to maximize the time they spend at home with the kids or just start some DIY projects.

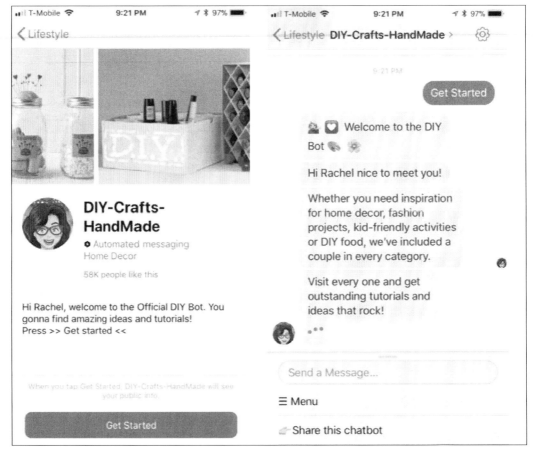

Figure 8: DIY-Crafts-HandMade FB Messenger bot

Voicebot examples

One of the limitations of today's voice-enabled devices is the voice itself. Whereas Google and Siri do offer a couple of voices to choose from, Alexa is limited to only one voice and it's very difficult to create that personality that we are looking for. While this problem probably will be solved in the future, as technology improves, I find the creativity of the insurance company GEICO around that very inspiring. In its efforts to keep its Gecko's unique voice and personality, GEICO has incorporated multiple MP3 files with a recording of Gecko's personalized voice, as a part of its Alexa skill.

Figure 9: Gecko's voice is a smart solution in a limited situation

GEICO has been investing in Gecko's personalization for years. Gecko is very familiar from TV and radio advertisements, so when a customer activates the Alexa app or Google Action, they know they are in the right place. To make this successful, GEICO incorporated the Gecko's voice into various (non-dynamic) messages and greetings.

It also handled the transition back to the device's generic voice very nicely: after Gecko has greeted the user and provided information on what they can do, it hands back to Alexa with every question from the user by saying, *My friend here can help you with that*. This is a great example of a cross-channel brand personality that also comes to life on automated solutions such as chatbots and voicebots.

Build an omni-channel solution – find your tool

Thinking less about the design side and more about the strategic side, remember that new devices are not replacing old devices: they are only adding to the big basket of channels that you must support. Users today are looking for different services anywhere and anytime. Providing a similar level of service on all the different channels is not an easy task, but it will play a big part in the success of your application. There are different reasons for that. For instance, you might see a spike in requests during the early morning and late night coming from home devices, such as Amazon Echo and Google Home. However, during the day, you will see more activity on FB Messenger or your intelligent assistant.

Different age groups also consume products from different channels and, of course, geography has a lot of impact as well. Providing cross-channel/omni-channel support doesn't mean providing different experiences or capabilities. However, it does mean that you need to make that extra effort to identify the added value of each solution, in order to provide a premium, or at least the most advanced, experience on each channel.

Obviously, there are differences between chatbot and voicebot interactions: we talk differently to how we write, and we can express ourselves with emojis, while expressing our feelings with voice is more difficult. There are even differences between various voice-enabled devices, such as Amazon Alexa and Google Assistant/Home and, of course, Apple's HomePod. There are technical differences but also behavioral ones: the HomePod offers a set of limited use cases that businesses can connect with, whereas Amazon Alexa and Google Home let us create our own use cases freely. In fact, there are differences between various Amazon Echo devices, such as the Echo Show, which offers a complementary screen, and Echo Dot, which lacks in screen and in sound in comparison.

With all that in mind, it is clear that developing a *good* conversational application is not an easy task. Developers must prove profound knowledge of machine learning, voice recognition, and natural language processing. In addition to that, it requires highly sophisticated and rare skills that are extremely dynamic and flexible. In such a high-risk environment, where today's top trends can skyrocket in days or simply be crushed in as little as few months, any initial investment can be dicey.

There are some developer tools today that offer multi-channel integration to some devices and channels. They are highly recommended from a short and long-term perspective. Those platforms let bot designers and bot builders focus on the business logic and structure of their bots, while all the integration efforts are taken care of automatically. Some of those platforms focus on chat and some of them on voice.

A few tools offer a bridge between several automated channels or devices. Among those platforms you can find Conversation.one (disclaimer: I'm one of the founders), Dexter, and Jovo.

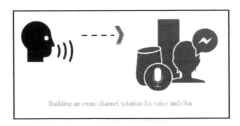

Building an omni-channel solution for voice and chat

Figure 10: Building an omni-channel solution for voice and chat

Stay up-to-date with the trends

While this is correct for any digital solution, conversational UI is an extremely new field in computing and it is also extremely dynamic. As such, today's top trends might become huge, but they might also become obsolete and outdated in just a few months. Listen to your clients and make sure that you are providing them with what they expect. Learn from others (learn even from your competitors) and evolve as technology improves and reaches new heights. This includes paying attention to new NLU capabilities, as well as the capabilities of devices and channels. This also includes supporting new types of enabled conversations; adding new functionalities, relevant UI and UX; and, of course, supporting all of the latest popular devices.

Many things that weren't available just a few months back have now become the backbone of some of the leading services. This includes the option to choose between different voices, the ability to build contextual interaction, and the possibility of creating a multi-step intent. Analyze and measure your bot's functionality: see how many people it has helped and where it has failed. Is it really replacing a human agent? Is it really generating new leads or any value that is measurable?

Keep yourself informed about new trends and capabilities in relevant publications. I recommend following `Voicebot. ai`, *Chatbot Magazine*, *Chatbot Life*, and the Artificial Intelligence section on *D-Zone,* and looking for relevant publications based on your segment/vertical.

Summary

To sum up the recommendations of this chapter in a few words, I would say that your bot must offer real value and provide rich functionality. Your automated solution, whether through voice or chat, consumed from any channel that the user approaches it from, is a tool for your business to provide a service and value for your customers at scale. The bot is not your goal – it's a tool. It's an additional communication interface that you should leverage to maximize your business goals.

You can start with small, experimental bots, but we are already at a stage where bots should provide a search engine experience and act less like a command line. Think what you need to achieve with your bot. Which NLU or development platform are you using to achieve those goals? Make it an ongoing process: it's not a one-time project! Grow with this exciting and dynamic market and try to be creative or a leader in your space. Everything is possible, so vision it and realize it.

We also talked about being sincere with customers: don't pretend that the bot is a real human, but give it the personality that best characterizes your business, through visual, semantic, and even voice methods. Last but not least, start now. Don't hesitate. Find the value that you can provide using voice-controlled and conversational capabilities and start building your bots.

In the next chapter, we will start with a technical drilldown on how we develop Amazon Alexa skills and Google Actions.

References and additional reading

https://www.nice.com/engage/blog/Everybody-Hates-IVR-2183

https://chatbotsmagazine.com/

https://www.voicebot.ai/

https://chatbotslife.com/

https://dzone.com/artificial-intelligence-tutorials-tools-news

～ 4 ～

DESIGNING FOR AMAZON ALEXA AND GOOGLE HOME

In *Chapter 2*, *How Not to Build Your Next Chat and Voicebots*, we talked about the emergence of voice solutions over the last couple of years and the differences between designing chat and voice applications. We saw that even though voice is not new to us, its capabilities until recently were limited mostly to IVR systems and recorded messages. It was far from being a *conversational* communication, but with new voice-enabled devices, including Amazon Echo and Google Home, things started shifting.

In *Chapter 3*, *Building a Killer Conversational App*, we looked at five tips for building a killer conversational application reflecting both voice and chat applications.

In this chapter, we will focus on voice design and, more specifically, on Amazon Alexa and Google Home. We will review both technical and voice UX recommendations and provide some examples. We will start by reviewing the different devices and operating systems, and will dive deeper into building an Alexa skill and a Google Home action. This step-by-step guide will help you to set up your first conversational application on those two channels.

Amazon Echo? Alexa? Google Home? Actions? What does it all mean?!

We have talked about voice applications and voice-enabled devices, but before we continue our drilldown, let's start with a quick overview to better understand the various terms and solutions that are available on the market today. We will start with Amazon's products and then talk about Google's products, and we will devote a short section to Apple's HomePod as well.

Amazon Echo

Amazon Echo, frequently shortened and referred to as Echo, is a brand of smart speakers developed by Amazon. Some reports state that Amazon has been developing Echo devices since 2010, as part of its first attempts to expand its device portfolio beyond the Kindle (https://en.wikipedia.org/wiki/Amazon_Echo).

The first-generation Amazon Echo, released in 2015, consists of a 23.5 cm tall cylinder speaker, with a seven-piece microphone array, and it requires a wireless internet connection to work. In the default mode, the device listens to all speech, monitoring for the wake word ("invocation word") to be spoken. Echo's microphones can be manually disabled by pressing a mute button to turn off the audio processing circuit.

Figure 1: Amazon Echo responding to a request by showing blue light signals

Echo Dot

In March 2016, Amazon introduced a smaller version of Amazon Echo, coined as Amazon Echo Dot (it has the shape of a hockey puck), the purpose being to make it easier to use in bedrooms as an alternative to the full-sized Echo. Apart from its size, Amazon stated that there are no differences between the original Amazon Echo and Dot. Having said that, it has been noticed that the full-size Amazon Echo's speaker is more powerful, while Dot is more sensitive to background noises.

Figure 2: Echo Dot, a hockey puck-sized device (www.cnet.com)

Echo Show

In May 2017, Amazon introduced Echo Show, bringing screens back to voice devices. With a 7-inch LCD screen, Echo Show unrolled new capabilities such as playing media (one of the most-used actions was playing YouTube while playing media, so as a response Google disabled YouTube on the Show device only a few months later) and making video calls.

Figure 3: Echo Show is reconnecting screens to voice

In 2017, Amazon released additional devices, including Echo Look and Echo Tap, as well as Echo Spot. All have similar functionality to the original Echo device.

Who or what is Alexa?

Alexa is the so-called "brain behind the machine." Alexa is the voice service behind the Amazon Echo, with whom we speak and (potentially) converse. Alexa started out by responding to simple user commands about home activities, such as turning on lights or opening the garage door, but over time Amazon opened Alexa up to other developers, enabling them to build "Alexa skills." Alexa skills are simply applications that trigger Alexa and are connected to the Echo devices.

Alexa is cloud-based and is already available on tens of millions of Amazon devices, as well as those from third-party device manufacturers. In March 2018, the number of skills on Amazon Alexa surpassed 30,000! With many developers looking to take advantage of these extremely fast-growing virtual assistant capabilities, Amazon took over both the smart speakers market (80% of the market) as well as the applications market (Google's numbers are around the 2,000 applications mark).

Google Home

Amazon's first-mover advantage resulted in an imposing 94% market share by Q3 2016. However, since then, Google Home has shown some growth in the market, reaching a little over 34%. Some predictions show that Google Home will take over Amazon Alexa by 2022 (see the following graph).

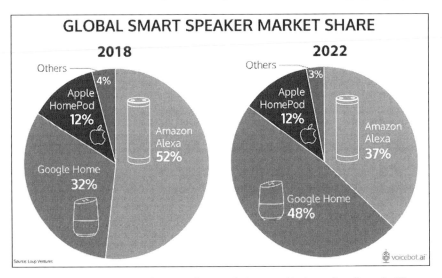

Figure 4: The smart speaker market and the predictions for Google Home (from `Voicebot.ai`)

Google Home is the brand of smart speakers that is developed by Google. The first device was released in the United States in November 2016.

Figure 5: The Google Home: a late bloomer?

Google Home's speakers, just like its competitors, enable users to speak voice commands to interact with services. The voicebot behind Google Home, which takes the form of an intelligent personal assistant, is called the Google Assistant. The Google Assistant is also available on most of the new Android phones and can be downloaded on Apple's devices.

In the same way as Amazon Alexa does, Google Home offers both in-house and third-party applications called **actions**. The actions allow users to interact with Google Home entirely by voice. Google Home devices also started with support for home automation, letting users control smart home appliances with their voice.

The original product has a cylindrical shape, with colored status LEDs on the top for a visual representation of its status. The cover over the base is modular, with different color options offered through the Google Store, which are intended to help the device to blend into the environment. In October 2017, Google announced two additions to the product lineup: Google Home Mini and Google Home Max.

Google Home Mini

Google Home Mini was announced and released late in 2017. Compared to Echo Dot, Google Home Mini is in many ways just like its competitor, coming with the same overall functionality but just in a smaller, donut-shaped size of 10 cm. Google markets the Mini with the slogan "Size of a donut. Power of a superhero."

Figure 6: The Google Home Mini: a response to Dot? (www.cnet.com)

Google Home Max

This is a larger version of Google Home, with stereo speakers, an audio connector, and a USB. Aiming to fight back against Apple's HomePod, Home Max includes Smart Sound, an adaptive audio system that uses machine learning to automatically adjust sound output based on factors such as the environment and time of day.

Figure 7: Google Max uses machine learning for Smart Sound (`www.target.com`)

Just a few words on Apple's HomePod

HomePod is Apple's smart speaker. It was announced the most recently (June 5th, 2017) and released in early 2018. Apple claimed that it delayed the release as it was investing its efforts in unique speaker capabilities. Without a doubt, the HomePod speakers are far better than the others. However, with a substantially higher cost ($350 compared to $30-$80 for its competitors), together with its minimal functionality, HomePod is losing the fight.

Many people claim that Apple, which pioneered the voice market with Siri, has ended up missing out on the smart speakers market. Apparently, having Siri, Apple's voicebot, spread out on every iOS device wasn't a good enough springboard to take over the market for smart speakers from the beginning. That's okay because Tim Cook, Apple's CEO, claims that Apple cares less about being the first and cares more about being the best. However, even after its release, critics were much less enthusiastic about HomePod. While HomePod's sound capabilities are much better that its rivals, many people claim that it is simply not smart enough.

As opposed to its competitors, Apple also took a more closed approach, allowing developers to develop minimal capabilities within a closed scope of pre-configured options. This basically means that businesses can only connect their APIs to specific capabilities, rather than develop a unique user experience with their clients.

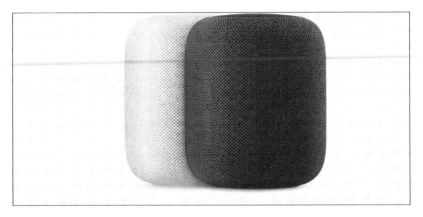

Figure 8: HomePod has great sound, but it is not so smart (www.apple.com)

Developing skills and actions

Both Amazon and Google see the value of the developer community as the key to the success of their voice assistants. As such, the two platforms offer development consoles that let developers build and deploy voice applications. In this section, we will focus on the set of tools offered by the Amazon Alexa Developer portal and the Google Assistant, and offer a step-by-step tutorial to get started.

Whether building an Amazon Alexa skill or a Google Home action, those kinds of applications are built to provide answers to the user's requests. With this in mind, when building those skills, we should think of them as being in a Q&A format. This means that we will figure out what the user will say or ask, and then what the response should be.

Here is a simple example: a user says, *I need help with my insurance.*

Your skill/action responds, *Please call us at 1-800-1234-567.*

When we analyze the preceding request and response, we build them into the following plan.

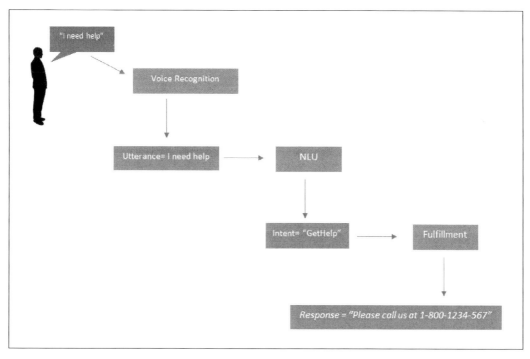

Figure 9: The technology journey of voice interactions

Voice recognition

Voice recognition (also known as speech recognition or speech-to-text) transcribes voice into text. The computer captures our voice with a microphone and provides a text transcription of the words. To read more about voice recognition, please see *Chapter 1, Conversational UI is our Future.*

Utterances

An **utterance** ("sample utterance" on Amazon Alexa or "user says" on Google Assistant) is a sentence that a user uses to ask a question or make a request. In the preceding example, *I need help* is our utterance.

One of the challenges of conversational applications, and voice in particular, is the need to plan all of the possible sentences and combinations of utterances for a specific **intent** (see the following section), and the possibility of mapping them correctly. In the preceding example, additional utterances could be:

- *How can I contact someone regarding my insurance?*
- *Who can help me with my insurance?*
- *I need assistance with my current insurance*
- *How can I call you regarding my insurance?*

There are many more possibilities. In fact, both Amazon and Google recommend providing at least 30 utterances for each intent, in order to make sure that the mapping between the user's request and the relevant intent is done successfully. Based on my experience, a couple of hundred, and sometimes even a thousand or more utterances, will provide a good accuracy rate.

Natural language understanding (NLU)

The NLU fulfills the task of reading comprehension. The computer reads the text (in a voicebot, it will be the transcribed text from the speech recognition) and then tries to grasp the user's intent behind it. To read more about NLU, please see *Chapter 1, Conversational UI is our Future*.

Intent

The user's goal is called their intent. The intent is based on the user's request. In the preceding example, the user requested help, so their intent was to get someone to help them.

Fulfilment

This is the code (API) that connects the intent with the required response.

Response

This is the answer we send back to the user. A response can be static, that is, hard-coded, like the phone number in our example, but it can also be dynamic. When providing a dynamic answer, we are able to customize/adapt the response based on specific parameters that the system collects (see entities/slots). To provide a dynamic response, we will also be required to connect the requests to a certain set of APIs.

Slots/entities

Slots/entities are used to create a more complex structure that provides more than just one question and one answer. To follow our example, let's say that the support phone number is based on the client's specific need. In this case, the user may say:

♦ *I need help with my* **car** *insurance*

♦ *I need help with my* **home** *insurance*

♦ *I need help with my* **travel** *insurance*

As you can see, the client's intent remains the same — "GetHelp." Instead of creating multiple flows for each unique insurance, we simply customize it using entities. The entities in our case are:

♦ **Car**

♦ **Home**

♦ **Travel**

This way, we can map the response, based on the entities we identified:

♦ GetHelp {car} → *Please call us at {CarNumber}*

♦ GetHelp {home} → *Please call us at {HomeNumber}*

♦ GetHelp {travel} → *Please call us at {TravelNumber}*

Now that we know how and what a conversational flow is comprised of, it is time to see how it is done on Amazon Alexa and Google Home.

Developing skills on Amazon Alexa

Amazon provides a developer console for developers to build their Alexa skills. Recently, Amazon also launched Alexa Blueprint, which lets non-developers build "personal skills" for home and game use cases.

In this tutorial, I will focus on the stages to build an Alexa skill for business use cases.

1. **Create or sign in to your Amazon Developer account**: Before you can build your Alexa skill, you will need to go to the Amazon Developer portal (`http://developer. amazon.com/`) and open a (free) account. If you already have an account, just click on the **Sign in** button.

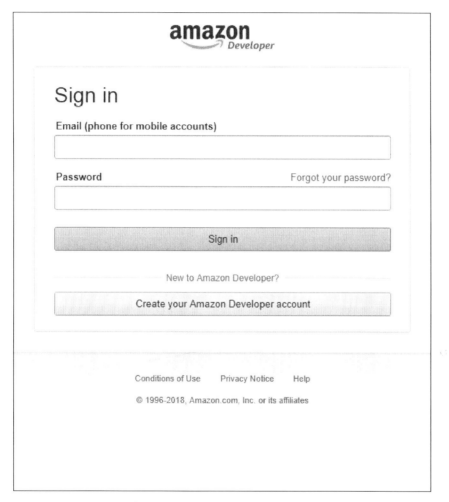

Figure 10: Developing a skill on the Amazon Developer portal

2. **Create your skill**: To start building your skill, click on one of the **Create Skill** buttons, as demonstrated in the following figure:

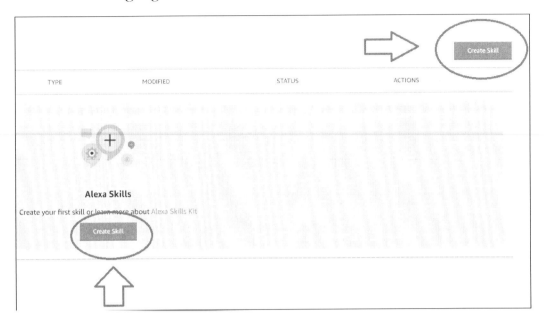

3. **Name your project**: Give your skill a name. This is still just the name of your project and not the name your users will use to start a conversation with your skill. In the following example, I named my skill "Packt Publication."

4. **Choose the skill's model**: Amazon Alexa offers a unique setup configuration for specific models, such as Smart Home and Video. Assuming we are building a skill from scratch here, I chose the **Custom** model option.

5. **Start customizing your skill**: Welcome to your skill's dashboard. On the left-hand side, you have the menu that walks you through the stages of setting up your Alexa skill, and on the right-hand side you have the four building blocks that build out your skill. These include:

   ◦ **Invocation Name**
   ◦ **Intents, Samples, and Slots**
   ◦ **Build Model**
   ◦ **Endpoint**

   We will review each stage in the following steps. Once done, all gray check marks will turn green and you will be able to launch your Alexa skill. We are almost there!

6. **Choose your invocation name**: Provide the name that will invoke your skill when the user approaches Alexa. In this example, I chose the same name as my project, however, it could be different. Amazon Alexa publishes the requirements for invocation names (see the green console in the following screenshot) and it is strict about them, mostly in order to make sure that they are not overlapping and that Alexa can understand them easily.

Among other stipulations, they can't be in capital letters, they can't use special symbols, and they must be more than just one word. Make sure you choose an invocation name that will make sense for your users but that will also comply with Amazon's requirements.

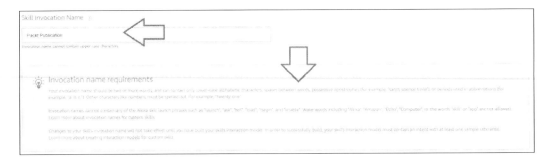

7. **Enable interfaces**: **Interfaces** are additional communication formats that you would like to enable on your skill. This includes audio or video players. Video players can only be enabled on Echo Show.

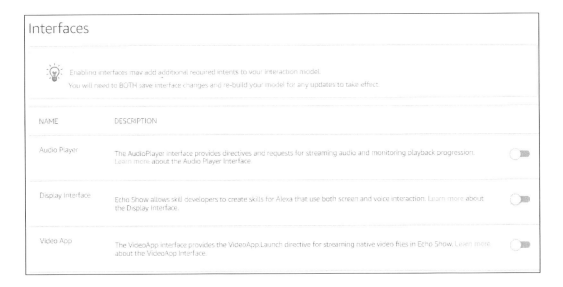

8. **Adding your intents**: Now we are at the core of building the skill – adding the intents. To begin, we provide each intent with a name. Make sure you use only non-capitalized letters and that words are connected (in case it's more than a one-word name). When done, click on **Create custom intent**. You will also see that Amazon provides common pre-made intents that you can use. It might be a good idea to start with the pre-made intents and then start building your own from scratch. Recently, Amazon Alexa enables to ask also for the user's phone number, which can assist when building a cross-channel interaction.

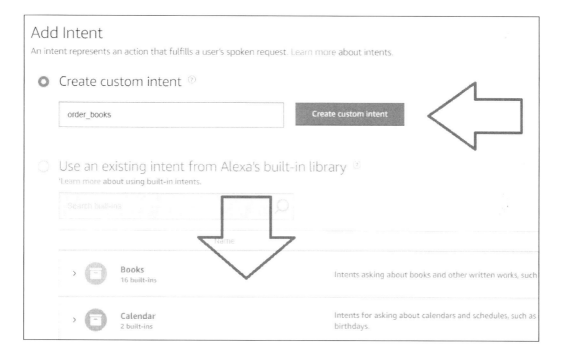

9. **Add your sample utterances**: As you may recall, each intent has a set of sample utterances that are, simply put, the sentences that users will say to ask for a specific request. The more we add, the higher the accuracy rate of the conversation. In our example, I added two samples that a user can use to order books. It is recommended to start with at least 15 samples. On this screen, you also have the option to add slots (as explained previously).

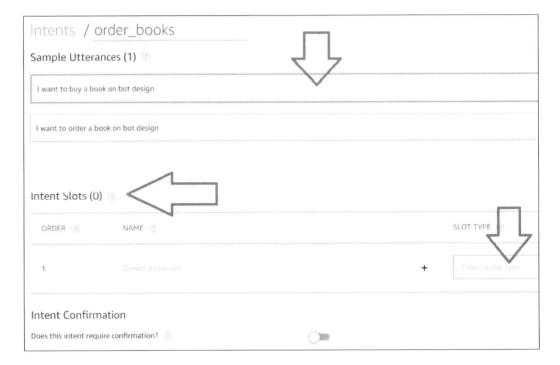

10. **Connecting your endpoint**: At this stage, we are connecting the intents and samples to the Lambda function we created. Choose the **AWS Lambda ARN** option and fill in the missing slots.

Note: In order for you to connect to Amazon Web Services (AWS) webservers, you are required to create a Lambda function using AWS. The AWS Lambda is where the code lives. When a user asks Alexa to use your skill, it is the AWS Lambda function that interprets the appropriate interaction and returns the conversation back to the user. I will not elaborate on how to build a Lambda function, but you can read a detailed tutorial for that here: `https://developer.amazon.com/alexa-skills-kit/tutorials/fact-skill-2**`

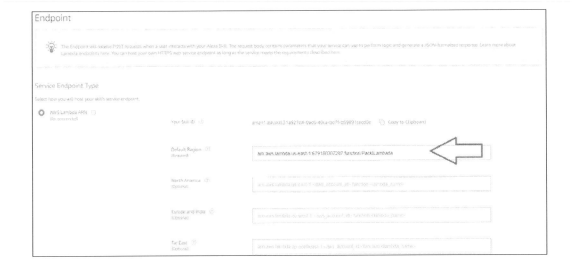

11. **Enter information on the Account Linking setting**: Amazon Alexa supports skills that require login, such as banking or retail. For this purpose, you will have to provide the account linking details that need to be verified when the user accesses the skill:

Account Linking

Do you allow users to create an account or link to an existing account with you?

Security Provider Information

Authorization Grant Type * ⑦	○ Implicit Grant ● Auth Code Grant
Authorization URI * ⑦	Enter URI...
Access Token URI * ⑦	Enter access token URI...
Client ID * ⑦	Enter client ID...
Client Secret * ⑦	••••••••••••••••••••••••
Client Authentication Scheme * ⑦	HTTP Basic (Recommended)
Scope ⑦	+ Add scope
Domain List ⑦	+ Add domain

12. **Enable permission request**: On the permission screen, we enable the option to ask the user for the address of the device, to provide them with geo-services information in a smart way. By knowing the address, we can provide location data for utterances such as *What is the closest sushi restaurant?* or *Please send me a new sample to my home.* The device's address is always available on each Amazon Echo device, as this is part of the device's setup process. Recently, Amazon Alexa enables to ask also for the user's phone number, which can assist when building a cross-channel interaction.

13. **You are (almost) done**: Remember the four building blocks we started with? As you can see, they are all checked now, which means that you have successfully completed the initial setup process!

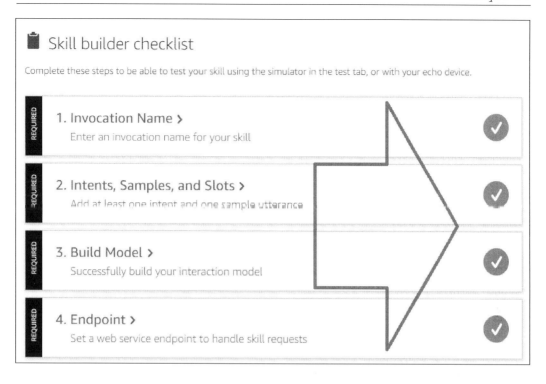

14. **It's time to test what we've built**: Amazon offers a wide set of testing tools for skills, from a real Alexa simulator to a manual JSON, as well as voice and tone (so that you can hear how things are pronounced). Take the time to test your skill and see that it's working. This is a good time to see whether you connected your endpoint correctly and whether your intents and sample utterances make sense.

15. Alexa also offers a beta-testing mode, which lets you share your skill with other testers before you push it to production. Invitations are sent by email and require (always!) the other tester's email address that is connected to his/her specific Echo device:

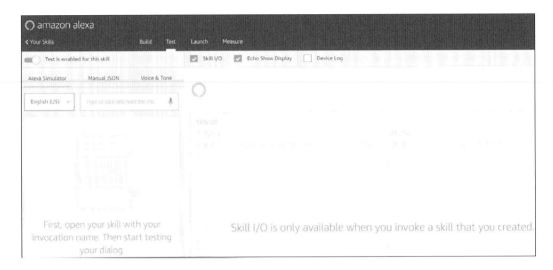

16. **Provide additional information on your skill**: The additional information on this page will be used for discovery and instructions once the skill is published to the public. As you can see, you are required to provide a description, icons in various sizes, and some examples to instruct the user on how to use the skill after they have enabled it:

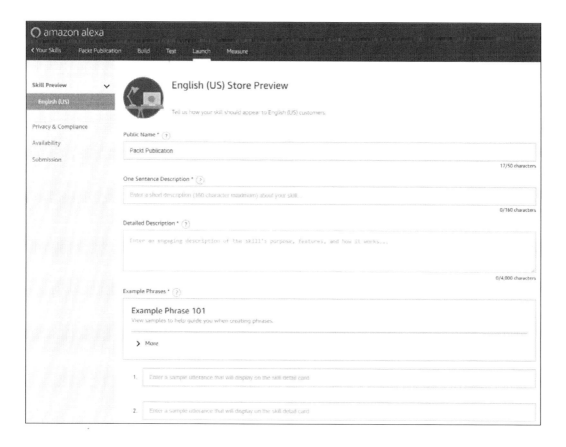

17. This information will then appear on your skill's page on the Alexa app, as you can see in the following Expedia page example:

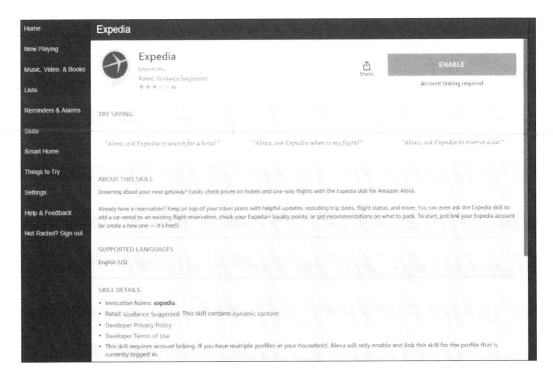

18. **Check your checklist before you can submit**: Understanding that there are quite a lot of steps here, Amazon Alexa provides a list of missing information or errors that must be corrected before you can submit the skill. Review them carefully, fix them, and refresh the page to get the most up-to-date status.

19. **Submit**: Congratulations, you are ready to submit your skill for review.

20. After you submit, the Amazon Alexa team will review and test the skill and will make sure that it is working properly. You must be patient though. This may take a week (and sometimes more). You will receive a notification when the review is completed, and in case changes are required, you will receive a detailed document with all the failures and suggestions on how to fix them (please note that for some categories, such as banking and retail, there are different submission procedures).

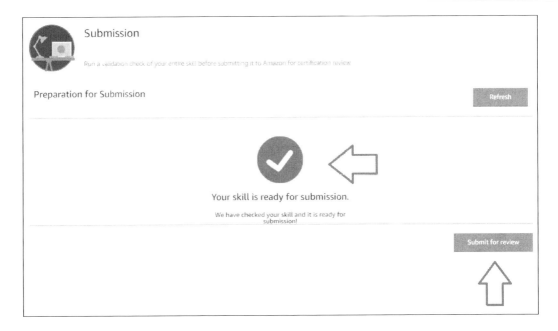

Developing actions for Google Home

Google provides a developer tool to build Google Home actions / Google Assistant applications. The underlying NLU on the Google Assistant is called **Dialogflow** (previously known as `api.ai`, which was acquired by Google in 2016).

In this tutorial, I will focus on the Dialogflow tool available for building conversational applications.

1. **Create your account or log in**: To start building actions, you will need to open an account on Google Actions. Visit `https://console.actions.google.com/` and use your Google account to log in. If needed, create a new free account.

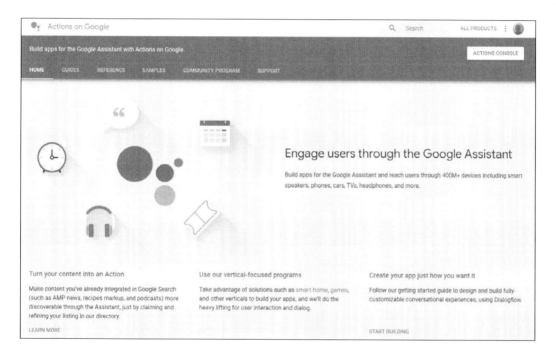

2. **Add/import your project**: To start a new project or import a project you have built separately, click on the large square box.

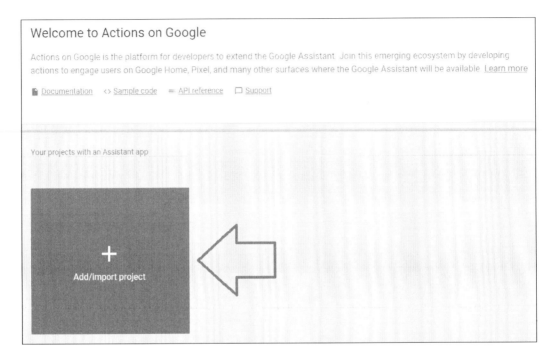

3. **Name your project**: Name your project and decide on the location. Once you have more than one project, you will have a gallery of projects that you can further build and manage. Pick a name that is relevant for the project, so it will be easy to follow up on. When done, click on **CREATE PROJECT**.

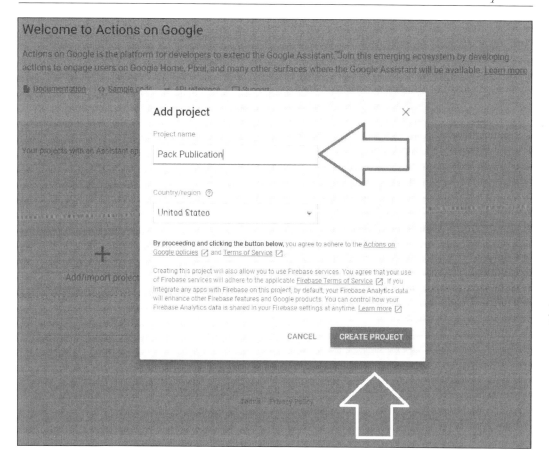

4. **Choose the type of action you are building**: Similar to Amazon Alexa, Google offers a set of pre-made actions/ intents that are connected to specific use cases, including home control, games, health, and more. Each of those categories offer ready-made apps, where you will only be asked to add your specific data. I recommend taking a look at these to understand how actions are built.

For the purpose of our demo, where we are building an action from scratch, we will click on **SKIP** at the top-right corner to get to the Dialogflow option, as presented in the following screenshot:

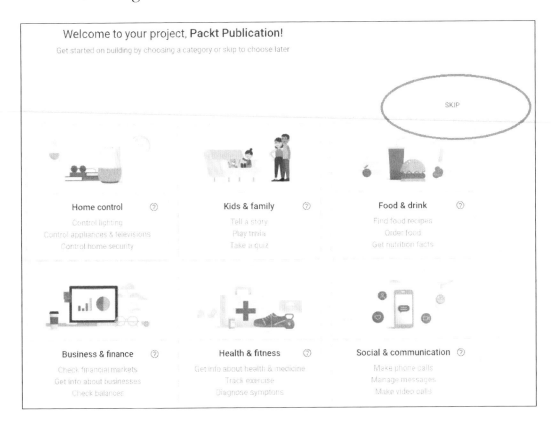

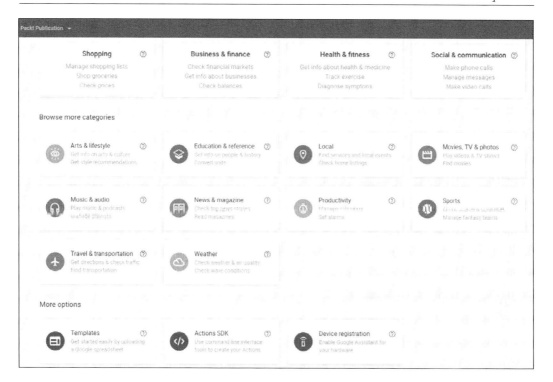

5. **Choose your invocation name**: After clicking on **SKIP**, you will land on your action's home page. We will start by clicking on **Decide how your Action is invoked** to configure the specific words people will use to start your action.

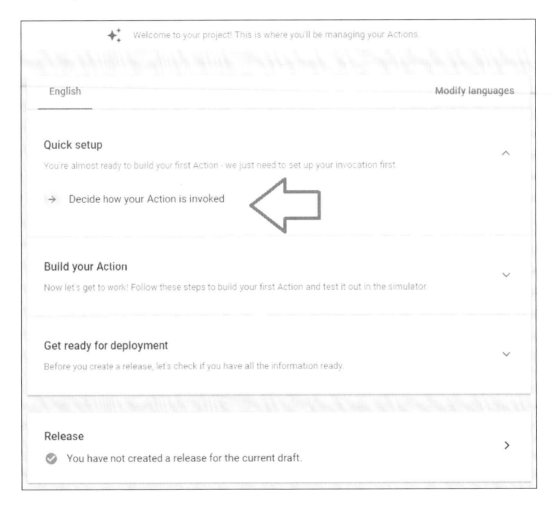

In the following example, we chose "Packt Publication." With this in mind, a user who will eventually ask to invoke our action will have to say, *Hey Google, talk to Packt Publication.*

We can also choose from a couple of male/female voices to represent our action, by choosing from the dropdown.

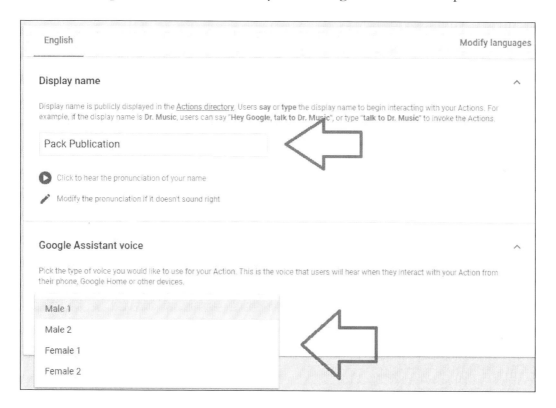

6. **Build your action**: It's time to build your app's business logic, which is mainly what people will be asking your action to do and how your app will react to it.

7. When done configuring, click on **Actions** under the **BUILD** section on the left-hand side menu (see the following screenshot) and then click on the **ADD YOUR FIRST ACTION** button.

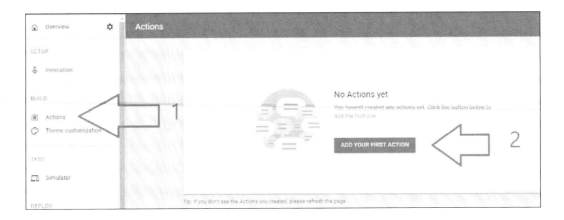

8. A pop-up window will prompt you to choose some of the pre-made/custom intents. If you don't find what you are looking for, click on **SKIP**. We click **SKIP** in this demo and continue to use Dialogflow.

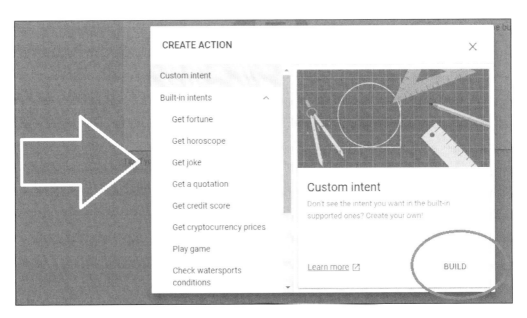

9. **Create your action**: On this screen, we can further tweak the project's name and, when done, we click on **CREATE**.

10. **Building your conversation**: As we demonstrated earlier, when building a conversational UI, we need to provide the questions that the user will ask and the responses they will get. To start the process, we will click on **CREATE INTENT** and start building our conversational flow.

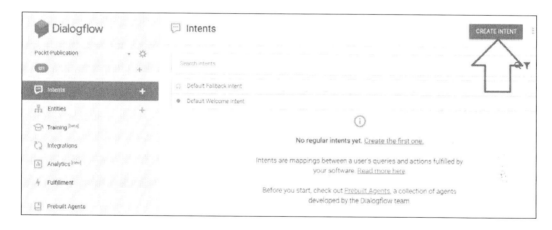

11. **Name your intent**: Provide a name for your intent, which will define the course of the conversation. I copied our previous example and created an intent related to ordering books and named it "OrderBooks."

12. **Fill in "what the user says"**: Start building in the questions from the user that could be relevant to this intent. The more samples we add, the higher the accuracy level of the conversation and the better the NLU succeeds at providing the right response. In the following example, I added only two sentences. It is recommended to start with at least 15-30 different sentences. Think of all the different permutations and options for a question that might be asked.

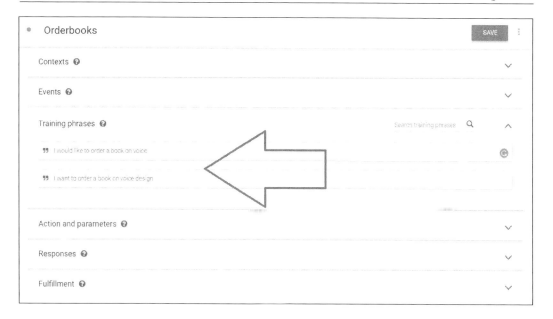

13. **Give the responses**: Similar to the examples we showed for Alexa, here, your responses can either be hard-coded as sentences or they can connect to a web service (API) and accordingly deliver a dynamic and personalized response, based on the user's request. In the following example, I provided three hard-coded responses to make sure that our bot is not acting monotonic. This means that if a user asks the bot the same question every day, they will receive slightly different answers, to make it sound less like a robot.

As mentioned before, if possible, it is highly recommended to use web services for responses.

14. **Integrations**: You can integrate your Dialogflow conversational UI with several services, such as Facebook Messenger, Slack, and others. To enable your conversational UI on Google Home, click on the large center-top rectangle, as shown in the following screenshot:

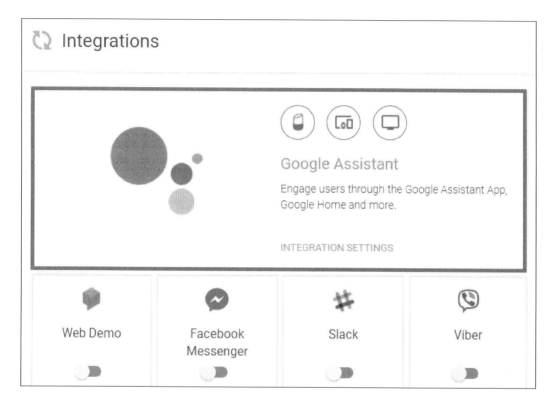

15. **Support additional languages**: Currently, Google Home and Assistant support more languages than Amazon Alexa, and Google is adding support for new languages as it grows. Among others, Dialogflow supports English (US, UK, GB, Canada), German, French, Japanese, and Korean. Google says that it will support 30 new languages in the next year.

16. **Your app's information**: On this screen, you are asked to provide the relevant app's information: pronunciation, description, images, and similar. This is very important for the discovery of your app, and on Google it works much better than on Amazon, since you can access any app from your Google Home with no need to specifically enable it.

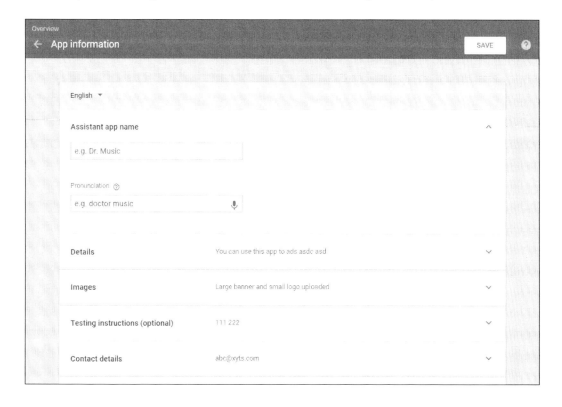

17. **Test your app**: You can either test in the simulator or talk to it to test your conversational application. A good test will include different variations of multiple samples and intents. The tool offers you a debug console, so if something does go wrong, you will have all the related information to fix it.

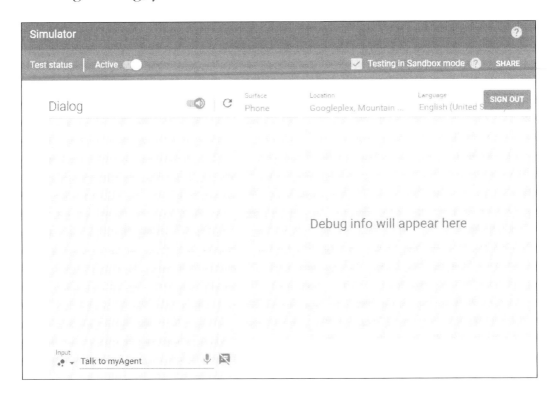

18. **Send it to world**: Once you have completed every stages, you can submit your action for review. The Google reviewers are relatively faster in their responses than the Amazon Alexa reviewers and you will receive a list of issues that you are required to fix before you can launch your application.

Ready? Click on **SUBMIT FOR REVIEW**.

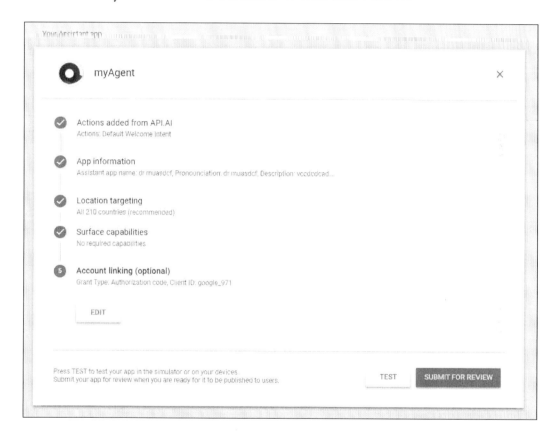

Summary

As you may have realized by now, building a voice-enabled application is a thrilling experience, however, it is not necessarily an easy task for non-developers, or even for developers. This is also true for the Amazon Developer console, as well as the Google Assistant / Home console. Today, those tools are not ready for non-developers and still require coding and programming on many different levels. To fill this gap, some startup companies, such as Storyline, PullString, and Jovo, provide simplified tools to build voice applications for Alexa. I would recommend referring to one of them if you are looking to build simple use cases that can be supported using a state machine (see more about the state-machine structure in previous chapters). Very few tools today provide a visual and simple interface for more complex use cases (my company, Conversation.one, included).

As voice UI and UX are just evolving, it only makes sense that those tools will change and evolve. I anticipate that in the near future, we will see both Google and Amazon providing more easy-to-use tools (such as Amazon's Blueprints) for self-developing purposes. It will be interesting to see how those two companies attract small and large businesses with tools that require no/very little development effort.

In the next chapter, we will focus on Facebook bot design: the tools to use, and the experience we can expect to achieve.

References

♦ https://en.wikipedia.org/wiki/Amazon_Echo

♦ https://www.voicebot.ai/2018/03/22/amazon-alexa-skill-count-surpasses-30000-u-s/

♦ http://www.visualcapitalist.com/smart-speaker-market-share/

♦ https://www.voicebot.ai/2018/02/12/google-smart-speaker-market-share-leader-2022-homepod-pass-20-million-units/

♦ https://en.wikipedia.org/wiki/Google_Home

♦ https://www.engadget.com/2018/02/13/apple-homepod-review/

♦ http://www.trustedreviews.com/reviews/apple-homepod

♦ Alexa Blueprints: https://blueprints.amazon.com/

♦ Amazon Alexa app: https://alexa.amazon.com

♦ Google acquires api.ai TechCrunch: https://techcrunch.com/2016/09/19/google-acquires-api-ai-a-company-helping-developers-build-bots-that-arent-awful-to-talk-to/

♦ Google Home will support more languages: https://techcrunch.com/2018/02/23/google-assistant-will-support-over-30-languages-by-year-end-become-multilingual/

~ 5 ~

DESIGNING A FACEBOOK MESSENGER CHATBOT

Chatbots and voicebots both fall into the conversational UI category. In the previous chapter, we talked about designing and building voice user experience and interface. Next, we will go back to the design of textual bots, focusing on the **Facebook** (**FB**) Messenger platform. With the promise of enabling a "connection to 900 million people on the Messenger platform" and with the goal to "take over sales and customer service functions," FB has the target of revolutionizing the world of chatbots. Indeed, FB revealed at the F8 2018 conference that its platform runs 300,000 bots (`https://venturebeat.com/2018/05/01/facebook-messenger-passes-300000-bots/`), with more than 8 billion messages sent each day! This is four times more than in 2017.

Around 200,000 developers have used the FB Messenger platform to enable their bots, and that number continues to grow. FB puts a lot of emphasis on the Messenger platform and continues to add features and capabilities to attract developers to its platform, such as menus, buttons, and cards, as well as rich media.

In this chapter, we will gain an understanding of the structure of the FB Messenger platform, its advantages, and its disadvantages. We will also work through a tutorial on how to build a FB Messenger bot using its internal tools and discuss other tools that are commonly used by developers in the market.

The FB Messenger stack

In *Chapter 1, Conversational UI is our Future*, we outlined the building blocks of conversational applications, focusing on speech recognition for voicebots, which is less relevant in the FB Messenger use case, and the need for a strong NLU component to understand the user's intent. The NLU, as we defined, fulfills the task of reading comprehension. The computer reads the text and then tries to grasp the user's intent behind it.

To accomplish this capability, in 2015, FB acquired `Wit.ai`, which is a speech recognition and natural language processing service. While originally, the goal was to take advantage of the voice recognition capabilities and voice interface APIs of `Wit.ai`, it ended up becoming the NLU engine of FB Messenger, improving the understanding level of bots within the Messenger platform.

Building a FB Messenger bot using Wit.ai

For this example, we will provide the user with a way to order this book. This is very similar to the process we followed on the voice-enabled devices in *Chapter 4, Designing for Amazon Alexa and Google Home*, and includes the NLU and the fulfillment components as well, which you can see as follows:

- A user says, *Where can I order a book on voice and chat design?*
- Your FB Messenger bot will respond, *You can purchase it online or in stores*

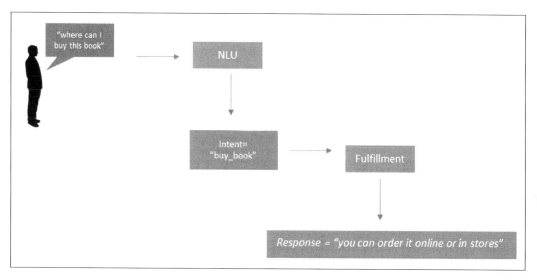

Figure 1: The conversational flow on FB Messenger

For a more detailed explanation of the flow, please refer to *Chapter 4, Designing for Amazon Alexa and Google Home.*

Tutorial

The following tutorial is built on the `Wit.ai` platform. I find `Wit.ai` a less friendly platform for non-developers and bot builders, however, this is the built-in solution offered by FB today. At the end of this chapter, I will refer to other solutions available on the market that you should be aware of. Let's get started!

1. **Sign in to your Wit.ai account**: Using a FB login or a GitHub login, sign in to the `Wit.ai` account. As you can see, `Wit.ai` is the NLU also supporting FB's mobile apps, home automation wearables, and robot solutions. In this tutorial, we will focus on building bots.

2. **Start building your bot**: In a very simple approach, the `Wit.ai` service's Messenger platform journey starts with training your bot by feeding in sentences and questions to it and connecting them to the relevant intent. Start by entering the questions the user will ask. In this example, we chose "Where can I buy a book on bot design?" Then create an intent to map this question to. We called our intent **buy_book**. To complete this stage, click on **Validate**. Add more and more "examples" to the sentence, to increase the level of understanding of your bot, and run through the same process, connecting it to the relevant intent.

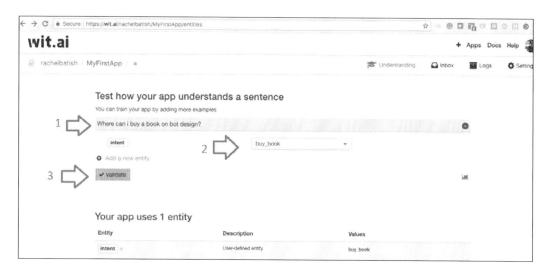

3. **Check the list of examples you've built**: Click on **Intents** to view the list of examples you have built into the bot. In this case, we have one intent, with multiple examples to support the accuracy level.

4. **Test your intent**: Now you can test your bot via the `Wit.ai` API: go to the **Settings** tab (marked with 1 in the following screenshot), then type one of the examples you have entered, such as "Where do I buy a Book on chat design?" Next, copy the curl box.

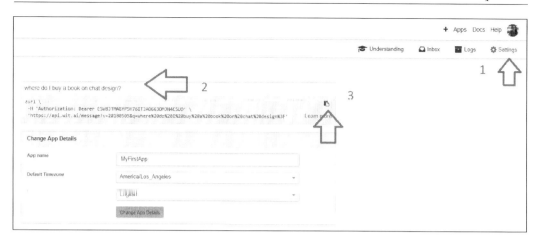

To make sure the request is mapped to the relevant intent, paste the curl in your terminal. You can see that the request was mapped to the right intent – **buy_book**.

5. **Continue to train your bot**: Go to the **Inbox** tab and see all the examples you tried when you tested the APIs. We can see, in the following example, that "Where do I buy a Book on chat design?" was correctly captured by the NLU engine.

For examples that were wrongfully mapped to intents, you can then create new intents and re-map them. In the following example, the user was asking where they could get coffee. The NLU engine mapped it to our **buy_book** intent (see screenshot).

Now, whenever someone asks for coffee, the system will already be able to identify the request and map it to the right place. We can test it again, by going back to the **Settings** tab and entering our new example in regards to ordering a coffee.

Now, we repeat the process by copying and pasting the curl into our terminal. In the following screenshot, you can see that the NLU was able to map the "where can I buy coffee?" question into our new **buy_coffee** intent.

When you are done re-mapping all intents, you will see that your inbox is empty.

6. **Configure the responses**: Your bot can now understand the difference between buying a book or a coffee, so the next step will be to connect those questions to your business logic and provide answers to the different questions. `Wit.ai` offers various ways to connect your business logic to your bot with different clients, including:

   ◦ The Node.js client (`https://github.com/wit-ai/node-wit`)

   ◦ The Python client (`https://github.com/wit-ai/pywit`)

   ◦ The Ruby client (`https://github.com/wit-ai/wit-ruby`)

7. **Integrating your bot with the FB Messenger platform**: This is the last stage of building a FB Messenger bot. In this stage, we will connect our bot with the Messenger platform, informing it that our bot will answer the questions for us (instead of a person). Calling to our bot is done from the app's "messenger settings" page. To do so, you have to connect your FB page and app and enable the NLU. Start by going to your app's "messenger settings" page and select the required subscribed pages in the "built-in NLP" section.

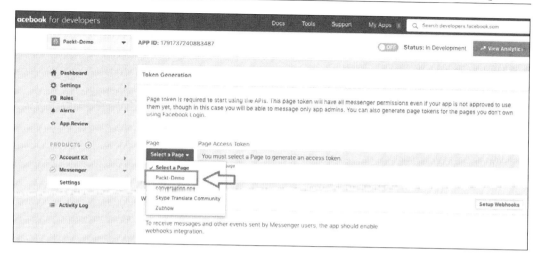

Last, add your Wit Server access token (find it on the bot's "settings" tab), as well as the callback URL you've configured, to fetch your business logic and save your settings.

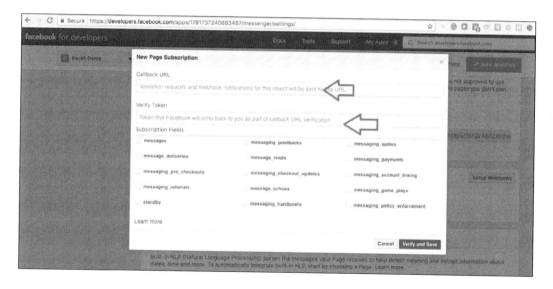

Congratulations! Your bot is ready to respond to your customers!

Challenges and consequences of the FB Messenger bot

The `Wit.ai` platform offers a tool to build an initial bot, where businesses can communicate with clients and offer services automatically. Like other solutions that we've discussed, when complexity is involved in interactions, those tools are very limited and heavier programming is required.

The integration and connectivity between the various stacks are also not easy to use and require a deeper development background. In addition, while being able to learn from a user's request using the inbox panel is of great value, the problem is usually when you have thousands or tens of thousands of requests running through the system, and a manual detection and re-mapping is nearly impossible.

In fact, FB itself shared that 70% of its automated bot interactions fail. A failed conversation means that the end user didn't get what they were asking for. While improving the NLU capabilities is a rather large task, FB decided to deal with this situation by offering a more graphic user interface, which includes menus and cards. Departing from the human-to-human interaction model that bots were meant to fulfill, the FB bot experience takes us back to the traditional graphic web experience, where end users are asked to choose from a pre-defined menu, instead of holding a "conversation" with the bot.

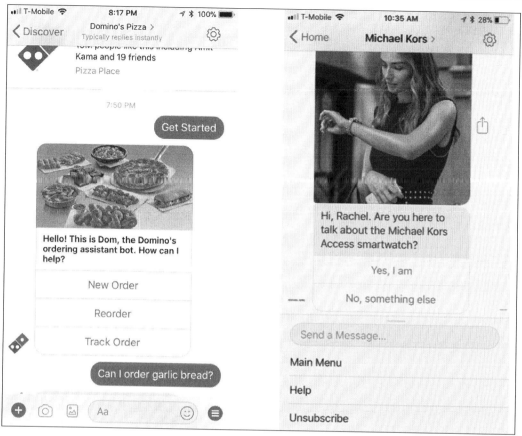

Figure 2: Choosing from menus, instead of conversing with a human-like bot

Is there a difference between bots and the web? In my opinion, this decision by FB has set the bot bar too low and has pushed back conversational UI interactions and expectations. Being the largest platform in the bot development industry, Facebook has had a negative impact on how bots are built. On the one hand, it has made it easier to build them, requiring uncomplex NLU development and level of understanding. However, on the other hand, it has brought us back to the web-surfing experience, putting the entire bot's essence into question.

Other tools to develop FB Messenger bots

FB's tool for building FB Messenger bots is not optimal. With the growing need to ease the process and enable a faster bot development process, which requires little to no development skills, various startup companies have developed visual solutions. In most cases, those solutions offer little to no NLU support, and follow the menu-based UI and UX that is promoted by FB.

Some of the platforms that are offering bot development tools for FB Messenger are:

- Chatfuel - `https://chatfuel.com/`

- Flow XO - `https://flowxo.com/`

- Botsify - `https://botsify.com/`

- Conversation.one - `https://conversation.one` (disclaimer: I'm a co founder of the company)

Summary

The FB Messenger platform offers developers and businesses a huge opportunity to communicate with their clients and increase their automated customer support and services, leveraging an existing communication environment that doesn't require the end user to get familiar with new technologies or solutions. However, the development tools that FB is offering today should become more mature and robust, and I expect to see a tighter integration of `Wit.ai` with the FB Messenger platform in the near future. FB's failure to provide an easy-to-use tool to develop its bots gave rise to some startup companies bridging this need by offering aesthetically pleasing and user-friendly interfaces that are available for non-developers as well.

While it started out with a great vision and mission, in practice, FB Messenger failed to deliver an advanced conversational experience and pushed the industry back into the classic web graphic UI, controlled by menus and pre-made selections.

As an industry leader, I believe that FB's role in shaping the future of bots will be immense and I hope to see it putting more emphasis on the NLU capabilities of the platform, to create true conversational experiences between machines and humans.

In our next chapter, we will talk about contextual design and how we can make our bots – via chat or voice – more human, and how they could eventually interact with us on multiple layers and not just through simple one-sided commands.

References

- https://venturebeat.com/2018/05/01/facebook-messenger-passes-300000-bots/
- http://www.businessofapps.com/data/facebook-statistics/
- https://venturebeat.com/2016/09/04/facebooks-seth-rosenberg-on-bots-business-and-the-future-of-messenger/
- https://mashable.com/2015/01/05/facebook-buys-wit-ai/#hAod20CoQiq4
- https://techcrunch.com/2017/07/27/wit-ai-is-shutting-down-bot-engine-as-facebook-rolls-nlp-into-its-updated-messenger-platform/
- Wit.ai tutorials: https://wit.ai/
- FB for developers: https://developers.facebook.com

6

Contextual Design – Can We Make a Bot Feel More Human?

Whether through chat or voice, our interaction with bots is still very much based on a user's request and, thereafter, the bot's response. We have already raised the challenge of creating and building contextual conversation, but in this chapter, we will dive deeper to explore the full meaning of contextual design and its components, and give some tips on how to create contextual conversation.

Contextual conversations or contextual design?

To understand how we build contextual conversations, we should start with some dictionary definitions. Let's begin with the definition of the word "conversation" (which we have already dealt with in previous chapters) and then look at the word "context" versus "contextual":

Conversation: *Is an interactive communication between two or more people. The development of conversational skills and etiquette is an important part of socialization. The development of conversational skills in a new language is a frequent focus of language teaching and learning*

(`https://en.wikipedia.org/wiki/Conversation`).

Context: *The circumstances that form the setting for an event, statement, or idea, and in terms of which it can be fully understood* (Oxford Dictionaries).

In context: *Considered together with the surrounding words or circumstances* (Oxford Dictionaries).

Out of context: *Without the surrounding words or circumstances and so not fully understandable* (Oxford Dictionaries).

Contextual: *Depending on or relating to the circumstances that form the setting for an event, statement, or idea* (Oxford Dictionaries).

Or:

Depending on the preceding or following parts of a text to clarify meaning (Oxford Dictionaries).

From the preceding definitions, we can summarize that a contextual conversation is a conversation or communication between people that is built on specific circumstances, which are not necessarily fully understandable when presented separately. When we design a contextual conversation, we need to base it on a statement, event, or idea, which can help us to understand or clarify other messages.

As humans, our brain can understand various messages, coming in different formats and with different levels of directness. From a very early age, we learn to understand direct and indirect commands or requests and, as we grow, we can "read" and reach a conclusion about a specific situation based only on the partial information we receive.

Over time, we learn to understand explicit and, more importantly, implicit sentences. We can derive data or understanding from previously obtained information, and we can also foresee the different potential consequences arising from multiple possible situations.

Being able to hold a contextual conversation is one of the main differentiators between humans and automated solutions, such as bots. Now, this is not to say that bots can't have a contextual conversation, however, it is much more difficult to achieve. As we broaden the coverage of a bot's domain, there are a vast number of possible contexts that need to be pre-configured. Here, we also see technologies such as AI, ML, and DL playing a big part in achieving this.

Building contextual conversations: humans versus bots

Let's look at a few examples of possible conversations, to compare the interactions we have as humans to the ones we create for our bots. To demonstrate the path of digitizing contextual conversations, I chose the following three scenarios:

♦ Human agent-customer conversation (on the phone)

♦ Online (website) self-service research

♦ Chatbot/voicebot interaction

The context I chose for the conversation is a search for a family trip to Disneyland. With today's regulations and liability concerns, many human-agent interactions with customer service staff or customer support call centers are fully scripted and it actually feels like we are talking to a bot.

In the following example, I gave the human agent some more room for maneuver in their conversation with the customer and included some more contextual elements, which should eventually be achieved with an automated solution, to create a fully engaged conversation.

Scenario 1: Looking for a trip to Disneyland: human-human interaction.

In this case, the conversation is a phone call between a travel agent and a customer. There is a big difference between whether the customer is meeting face-to-face with the agent or talking over the phone/email, but to try and make the example as close as possible to web/bot interaction, I chose the phone (where we lack parameters such as appearance and facial mimicry).

Sub-scenario breakdown:

♦ The travel agent doesn't know the customer/anonymized interaction

♦ The travel agent knows the customer and has details about his/her family, that is, can make more assumptions, hence it is a personalized conversation

Scenario 1a – Anonymized interaction

Customer: *Hi, my name is Laura. Have I reached the Disneyland Travel Agency?*

Agent: *Hi Laura, you sure have reached us. My name is Nadine and I will be happy to help you today and make your Disneyland trip as magical as possible. When are you looking to travel? And how many days will you stay? We have some great one-week packages.*

Customer: *We are a family of five and we are interested in the three-day package.*

Agent: *OK, so two parents and three children, for a three-day package. And when did you say you were planning your vacation?*

Customer: *June.*

Agent: *Perfect, I have a few options for you. Let me know what could work best for you.*

Scenario 1b – Personalized interaction

Customer: *Hi Nadine, it's Laura. How are you?*

Agent: *Oh, hi Laura! How are you? I can't believe it's already that time of the year! How are the kids doing? Excited for their annual Disney magic? Is it going to be June again for your vacation this year?*

Customer: *Yes, time flies so fast! And it is June indeed. Do you have some new packages to offer us?*

Agent: *Sure, let me see what we have for our 'one-week magical package' this year.*

I found a couple of great deals for you with some 'extras' for the kids, now that they are a bit older. Let me know what could work best for you.

Scenario 2a – Anonymized web browsing

Travel web browsing has made great improvements over the years, providing us with great flexibility in terms of dates, locations, and price ranges. We are exposed to a great deal of options, which we can filter in order to find the best result. This is how it goes:

1. The customer uses a search engine on the web and ends up at `the-disneyland-travel-agency.magic.com`

2. They use the search bar to provides dates, the number of people, and in some cases some add-ons configuration to receive the most relevant results

3. Multiple results are presented, based on the customer's sort preference (cheapest, most popular, or other)

4. The customer may be offered the best deals/additional services based on their current search

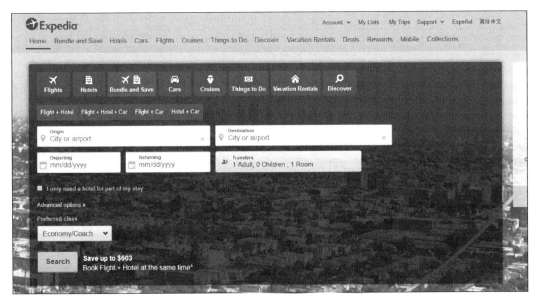

Figure 1: A typical travel search bar with required parameters to optimize results (from www.expedia.com)

Scenario 2b – Personalized web browsing

1. The customer logs in to their account at the-disneyland-travel-agency.magic.com.

2. Their preferences are known to the website and they are offered some tailor-made recommendations based on their recent purchases or searches. They are also offered the option to continue their last search, which they failed to complete on their previous visit.

3. They either continue their search or start a new one, providing dates, the number of people, and in some cases some add-ons configuration to receive the most relevant results.

4. A very large number of results are presented to the user, based on the customer's sort preference (cheapest, most popular, or other).

5. The customer is offered the best deals/additional services/ extra credits based on their account and profile details.

 Note: With the use of web cookies, we can offer personalized content even to anonymous users, so we don't necessarily require login for personalization.

Scenario 3a – Anonymized bot interaction

Bot: *Hi, I'm your Disneyland travel bot. How can I help you today?*

Customer: *We want to book a vacation to Disneyland.*

Bot: *Sure, I can help you with that. I just need you to provide me with a few details: when do you plan to travel?*

Customer: *June.*

Bot: *How many adults?*

Customer: *Two.*

Bot: *How many children?*

Customer: *Three.*

Bot: *Are you looking for a one-day, three-day, or one-week package?*

Customer: *Three-day package.*

Bot: *I found the following three options: 1) XXX 2) XXX 3) XXX.*

Customer: *Number three please.*

The bot completes the order/hands over to an agent.

Scenario 3b – Personalized bot interaction

Bot: *Hi Laura, I'm your Disneyland travel bot. How can I help you today?*

Customer: *I want to book a vacation to Disneyland.*

Bot: *Would you like to complete your previous order to Disneyland?*

Customer: *No, make a new one.*

Bot: *Sure, can you tell me when you plan to travel?*

Customer: *June.*

Bot: *How many adults?*

Customer: *Two.*

Bot: *How many children?*

Customer: *Three.*

Bot: *Are you looking for a one-day, two-day, or one-week package?*

Customer: *Three-day package.*

Bot: *I found the following three options: 1) XXX 2) XXX 3) XXX.*

Customer: *Number three.*

The bot completes the order/hands over to an agent.

 Note: Here as well, we can use web cookies and offer personalized content even to anonymous users, so we don't necessarily require login for personalization.

In the preceding example, we have included the matrix of a personalized versus anonymized interaction, and tested it on three channels:

♦ Human-human

♦ Human-web

♦ Human-bot

The following comparison table includes the advantages and disadvantages of the services as they are provided today:

	Human-human	Human-web	Human-bot
Availability	Low-medium: Based on the business opening hours/after-hours services and number of agents	High: 24/7	High: 24/7
Scalability	Low-medium: Based on number of agents	High: Can serve many customers in parallel	High: Can serve many customers in parallel
Conversational	High: Agent can make assumptions based on implicit and explicit parameters	None-low: Correspondence is highly structured and has to be very implicit	Medium-high: Depending on the bot and its maturity. Mostly structured based on the decision tree model.
Contextual	Medium-high: Depending on the agent	Low-medium: Based on given parameters, as well as cookies/account registration	Low: Today, most bots are still non-contextual, however, they can reach a higher level based on cookies/ account registration

Engagement level	Medium-high: Depending on the agent	Medium: Depending on prompts and capabilities to generate additional offerings based on personal data	Medium-high
Complexity level	High: Can deal with most/ all use cases	Medium: Depends on the coverage of use cases and options. The fallback is to a human agent.	Low-medium: Depends on the coverage of use cases and options. Most complex scenarios are not yet covered and the fallback is to the website/a human agent.
Focus	High: The agent will respond to the customer's needs based on the interaction	Medium: Web searches can lead to an "over-data" exposure situation. It can be difficult to navigate through all the information.	Medium-high: The bot acts like an agent and responds to the client's direct request. This helps to reduce the "noise" around the search/ action.

| Cost | High:

Increases as more agents are needed to respond | Low:

Servers/ developers/ designers | Low:

Servers/ developers/ bot designers

(10-15 times less than a human agent) |
| Customer's satisfaction rate | Medium-high | Medium-high | Low |

From the preceding table, we can see that the clear advantages of digitized solutions over human-human interaction are scale, availability, and costs. However, in terms of being able to hold a contextual conversation, web and bots are still very limited. We can conclude that with today's capabilities, human-human interaction should be used for complex tasks, whereas web and bot interactions make sense in more simple a, fast communication instances.

Even when we compare the web to bots, with their current capabilities, it is clear to see that the web is much more mature and is therefore also trusted by businesses and clients to a larger extent.

Online self-service tasks have replaced human-human interaction and the next step will be seeing conversational solutions, such as voicebots and chatbots, replacing the web and eliminating the need to search and browse for endless information. After all, when using a bot, we create a focused, narrow, and minimized approach, just as if we are talking to a human agent.

How can a bot be better than a web search or human interaction?

As mentioned, online self-service capabilities allow users to interact with flexibility and scalability 24/7. However, they tend to lack the "personal" touch and the "natural" interaction we are used to as humans, and they also overfeed us with information and data. It is difficult to navigate through this huge amount of data and there is a need to have someone/something filtering the data for us.

Understanding that human agents are costly and non-scalable, a bot's mission is to provide that human-touch interaction, screening the data for us and then getting us to the right place. However, a bot's experience today is rather scarce, being built on a decision tree model, which can end up being very frustrating. The sections that follow discuss the main differences between low-capacity bots and high-contextual bots.

Conversational structure

When we talk with a human, we can provide unstructured information and expect the human to understand our request and use the relevant parameters to provide us with the best option. Going back to our Disneyland example, to complete the purchase, we are required to fill in the following slots:

♦ Number of people

♦ Adults/children

♦ Number of days

♦ Dates

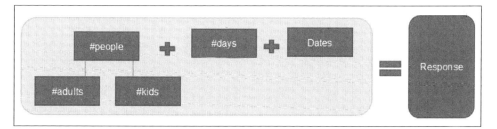

Figure 2: Data collection: structured versus unstructured conversation

In the human-human example, the customer outlined the following:

We are a family of five and we are interested in the three-day package.

From this sentence, the agent can fill in three slots based on this one question:

♦ Number of people: five

♦ Number of adults: two, and number of children: three

♦ Number of days: three

Missing data: dates.

In one follow-up question, the agent can fill in all the relevant slots to come up with a recommendation for the customer.

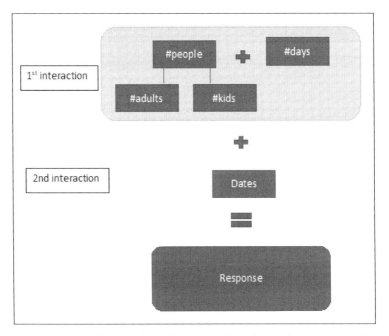

Figure 3: Data collection by a human: identifying the missing pieces

It took the human travel agent two interactions to collect all the data and provide a response. If we compare that with today's most common bot interaction, which is based on a decision tree, the bot is capable of collecting only one piece of information for each slot at a time, so the interaction would look as follows:

Customer: *We are a family of five and we are interested in the three-day package.*

Bot: *How many people?*

Customer: *Five.*

Bot: *How many children?*

Customer: *Three.*

Bot: *How many adults?*

Customer: *Two.*

Bot: *When would you like to travel?*

Customer: *June.*

Bot: *How many days are you looking to spend at Disneyland?*

Customer: *Three.*

Bot: *Here are all the options I found...*

As a response, the bot either provides a list/WebView or redirects to an agent.

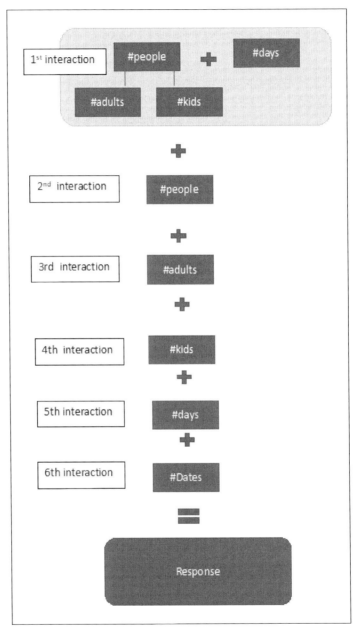

Figure 4: Data collection by a bot: using a decision tree process can create a poor experience

It took the bot six interactions to fill in the missing slots, in order to provide a list of options or, even worse, direct the user to a human agent. In many cases, if we would also like to ask for new dates, we would have to go through the entire process again. To create a positive human-like interaction, we should enable the user to talk and act freely, and make sure the bot collects the missing data.

In this case, the user is saying, *We are a family of five and we are interested in the three-day package.*

The bot should be able to fill in the relevant slots:

◆ Number of people: five

◆ Number of adults: two, and number of children: three

◆ Number of days: three

Then the bot should ask for the information for the missing slot: dates.

Programming such an interaction can be more challenging and requires an NLU engine that can deal with unstructured input and output. The NLU engine must be capable of understanding that the user is providing relevant data that fits certain slots. Naturally, the more complex the conversation becomes, and the more unstructured data is fed into the system, the more difficult it is to create such a natural flow without making mistakes. However, such behavior makes the interaction with the user more engaging and focused. This is when the user is more encouraged to use the bot, instead of leveraging an endless web search.

The user is now free to provide the information they had in mind and the bot can figure out the missing parts and ask specific questions. We have reached a contextual conversation of the highest possible level, equivalent to that of a person-person interaction, but in a way that is much more scalable and available.

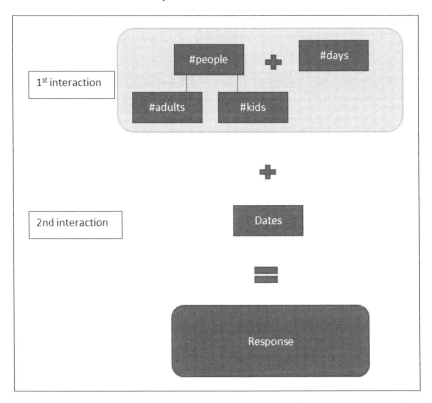

Figure 5: Data collection by a bot: automated contextual conversation in free flow

The bot as an intelligent assistant

One of the chatbot/voicebot's challenges is to provide the user with the the most optimal result it can, based on the parameters it was able to collect explicitly and implicitly. So, can a bot also make recommendations? Can it filter the data for the user?

Trying to provide a more human-like, conversational interaction with a chatbot or voicebot also means being able to filter the enormous amount of data that the user is used to consuming from his/her web-browsing experience. A good chatbot experience will not present us with an endless number of results (obviously this is not even possible when we think about a voicebot).

So, how can we filter 500 (or 5000!) options and give the user the one or two options that fit them best? How can we make sure our bot is advising users? The bot should not only collect information and reply to automatically configured questions, but should also come back with suggestions and recommendations that are specific and accurate for the user. This is where the bot becomes an intelligent assistant.

With the right level of NLU and a good level of understanding of the user's intents, both implicitly and explicitly, our bot can also help users to choose between several decisions and ultimately make the best one on their behalf.

The case of robo-advisors and how they impact the bot industry

The financial industry adopted the concept of **robo-advisors** in 2000. Robo-advisors carried out manual tasks and automated repetitive tasks on behalf of a person. Early robo-advisors were computer softwares used by (human) wealth managers in the financial industry. They served them by collecting information from their clients about their financial situation and future goals, and then using that data to offer advice and/or, eventually, automatically invest their clients' assets. It was all about automating processes, based on specific parameters, and coming up with the best recommendations or decisions.

With their consumerization, modern robo-advisors have completely changed the way investments are made by delivering the service straight to the consumer, eliminating the need to go through a wealth manager to make investments. Almost overnight, it was possible for everyone to handle their assets on their own.

Today, it is common to see the interface of robo-advisors as chatbots. Those intelligent assistants recommend certain actions and make decisions for customers automatically. They can also prompt users to take a certain action based on changing, dynamic parameters.

Robo-advisors, with their chat interface, are successful thanks to the exact same reasons we have outlined: they are less costly, they are accessible 24/7, and they provide results that are at least as good as those of a human wealth manager.

The concept of building an intelligent assistant, and not just a bot that collects data, is the next level of bot complexity and human-computer interaction. When building our bot, if we can combine the computerized capabilities of collecting, categorizing, and analyzing an enormous amount of data, together with the human brain's capabilities of making smart, calculated decisions based on that data, we can eventually turn a bot into a "superhuman."

Text and toning

As we outlined earlier in the book, the bot's goal is to replace human-human communication. The correspondence should be on a human level, and we went through the required parameters in this chapter as well as in previous ones.

In the next chapter, we will talk about how bots act compared to humans. What kind of "non-human" are they? What is their unique persona and how can we make the user trust them?

Before we build their personality, we should also think about how we can help our bots to understand not only the context of a conversation, but also its psychology and tone. In what emotional state is the user? Are they happy or angry? What is their tone like, based only on their text or voice?

This is called *emotional intelligence*. It is by far a less advanced field compared to AI, but it is one of utmost importance, especially for businesses who would like to make sure they understand the emotional status of their clients when they respond and interact with an automated solution. It can help them to navigate negative situations but can also positively boost sales.

Emotional intelligence versus AI-based emotional intelligence

According to the online magazine *Psychology Today*, emotional intelligence is the ability to identify and manage your own emotions and the emotions of others.

This includes three skills:

◆ **Emotional awareness**: understanding your emotions and the emotions of others

◆ **Harnessing emotions**: the ability to connect emotions and apply them to tasks

◆ **Managing emotions**: the ability to regulate your own emotions and to cheer up or calm down other people

(https://www.psychologytoday.com/us/basics/emotional-intelligence)

AI-based emotional intelligence is the attempt to develop a human capability for the bot to act on and navigate through the emotions of humans. With this in mind, the bot will be able to identify and detect emotional states such as happiness, anger, sadness, disgust, fear, and surprise.

After the bot detects the emotional context, it will respond to the feelings appropriately during the conversation. Some of today's AI-based emotional intelligence bots include the capability to detect facial expressions using a video camera when the bot corresponds with the other person on the other side. Voice analysis can help a bot to understand whether a person is angry or happy, but that can only be done by reading text or the user's vocal responses.

In fact, if we prepare in advance for the different ways our users may respond to us, there's a lot we can learn from them. I recommend preparing for three main scenarios when you are launching a bot, on top of the planned business logic of the bot:

+ **Positive responses:** when the user is happy or satisfied with the result

+ **Negative responses:** when the user is unhappy with the service they received

+ **Trolling**: when the user is trying to "mess" with your bot

Positive responses

Positive responses from a user are great for us. We know that the user is satisfied and we have successfully managed the interaction automatically. We can take advantage of positive responses to offer additional services or just reply nicely.

Example:

User: *Awesome, thanks.*

Bot: **You are welcome. Is there anything else I can help you with today?**

Or:

Bot: **I'm so happy I could help you! Anything else I can assist you with?**

You should be prepared to respond to positive feedback coming from the user with positive feedback. Think in advance about all the different ways a user might thank you or appreciate your response and provide alternate responses to keep the communication positive.

False-positive responses

Relying only on text, however, can be tricky and it is recommended that you take into consideration the conversation's context. It is very difficult to understand sarcasm or a cynical comment just from text, and without any unique voice-recognition capabilities, this is also true for voice.

Here is an example that happened to one of my colleagues, when a situation ended up going wrong: after unsuccessfully corresponding with a bot on a rather simple issue, my colleague gave up on the service and announced he was moving to a different provider. The conversation went as follows:

User: *Thank you so much, you really helped me get to a decision to move to {other company name}.*

Bot: **You are welcome! Is there anything else I can help you with?**

It is obvious that a human would have understood my colleague's intention much better, thanks to a couple of parameters:

◆ A human agent would have been aware of the context

◆ A human agent would have understood the sarcasm

◆ A human agent would have been familiar with the company's competitors

Having said that, I think that if this company had prepared better for negative feedback, it could have detected this specific sentence rather easily and transferred my colleague to a human agent immediately.

Negative responses

Negative responses from a user are a huge asset, if we identify them on time and can analyze and react to them correctly. I would say that it is even more important to prepare yourself for negative feedback than for positive feedback. A negative response means that the user is unhappy with the bot's responses, but it could also be that they are currently unhappy with the company's services in general.

Here is an example that includes both scenarios in one:

User: *My order didn't arrive.*

Bot: *Please provide me with your order number.*

User: *My order number is {xxxxx}.*

Bot: *I can't find this order. Is there anything else I can help you with?*

User: *I didn't receive my order.*

Bot: *Please provide me with your order number.*

User: *My order number is {xxxxx}.*

Bot: *I can't find this order. Is there anything else I can help you with?*

Use: *You are not helping me!*

Bot: *I don't think I can help you with this. Is there anything else I can help you...*

This conversation can go on and on until the client gives up. At this stage, the customer is unsatisfied because they 1) didn't receive their delivery and 2) are not getting the customer support they are looking for. The system should have analyzed the situation better by firstly detecting that the interaction with the client was in regard to a negative experience – an order that hadn't arrived – and been more sensitive to the client's emotional situation.

As a next step, the system should have identified that the bot wasn't able to provide the (angry/disappointed) user with a reply and should have seen if it could direct them to a human agent, or at least collected their contact details and offered for someone to call them back. In this scenario, as in the false-positive scenario, contextual conversation is highly important and its absence can cause lots of damage to the business.

Try to build your intents to include all possible scenarios of negative feedback, so that you can handle them correctly. Be prepared for the worse: people often use harsh words when they are unhappy.

Trolling

For some reason, people try to troll bots very often. This means that they deliberately and proactively try to offend them. Whether this is done to prove the other party is a bot, or to demonstrate that the bot is not smart, is of little importance. While it might take some effort on your side, I think that being prepared for trolling can bring back the user's trust and enthusiasm for your bot.

Example 1:

User: *Are you a bot?*

Bot: *Yes, I am.*

User: *You are stupid.*

Bot: *I'm actually pretty smart. What about you?*

When people try to identify whether the bot is a bot, they might ask some common questions:

Example 2:

User: *How much is 5+5?*

Bot: *It's 10 of course, however, math is not my specialty. Can I help you with {the service the bots can help with}?*

With a simple function that can calculate, and a sophisticated comment, you can bring back the user's trust and guide them back to a positive interaction.

If you are using an analytics solution that gives you an insight into what people are asking, take advantage of it to learn how they praise your bot, confront it, or question it. Understanding emotions is very difficult for us humans and it is even more so for computers. However, by monitoring and analyzing conversations, there's a lot we can learn and improve for subsequent conversations. Your bot will continue to evolve and expand its capabilities and a big part of that will be its emotional intelligence competences.

Summary

Making bots seem more human is the ultimate goal when trying to create them. With the goal of making them equivalent to humans, or for them to even replace humans for some of our daily tasks, expectations are high, which inevitably leads to some great disappointments. However, as we re-approach this new paradigm, we can understand that a lot can be achieved, even if with tiny steps.

In this chapter, we touched upon a bot's humanization process and its two necessities:

♦ Contextual interaction

♦ Emotional intelligence

Although not an easy task, building a bot while combining the two will ensure a successful experience for our users and a great learning experience for us, as the bot's owners.

Understanding contextuality is tough work even for humans, however, it is the key to creating a meaningful automated solution that can be expanded to even more use cases and opportunities. A bot that isn't capable of analyzing context will not survive long and will end up causing more damage than good to the business.

Emotional intelligence is yet another challenging area for humans, especially in today's digitized world. However, here we are expecting our bots and computers to understand emotions, react to them and manage them in the most humanizing way. AI-based emotional intelligence research is in its early days, but it will become very dominant in the next couple of years, as we continue our search to create humanized bots.

Although we use the terms "understand" and "feel" for bots, we clearly know that we are still in the teaching phase and very little, if any, self-teaching is done by today's computers and bots. However, as I've shown in the examples, there are multiple ways to prepare for different scenarios and, more importantly, to learn from past interactions in order to improve future ones.

Building your chatbot or voicebot is an ongoing process. It is a learning cycle in which both you and your bot will become smarter and more capable. Use all the methods that are available today on the market to help your bot to scale and grow, and remember technology moves fast – move with it!

References:

- *Robo-Advisor (Robo-Adviser) Definition | Investopedia*: `https://www.investopedia.com/terms/r/roboadvisor-roboadviser.asp#ixzz5G5Kc8P88`

- `https://www.psychologytoday.com/us/blog/behind-online-behavior/201607/the-psychology-chatbots`

- `https://chatbotslife.com/chatbots-are-getting-smarter-with-emotional-intelligence-9ea5cb573d54`

7

BUILDING PERSONALITIES – YOUR BOT CAN BE A BETTER HUMAN

In the previous chapter, we talked about how to make your bot seem more human: how it can better understand your customers, read between the lines, and hold a contextual conversation, which is more than only a request and a response flow.

In this chapter, we will talk about the importance of the personality of your bot, how to choose it, and what it should reflect when it's interacting with your clients.

Personification of computers

Personification is defined by Oxford Dictionaries as follows:

> *The attribution of a personal nature or human characteristics to something nonhuman, or the representation of an abstract quality in human form* (https://en.oxforddictionaries.com/definition/personification).

We are not new to the personification of computers. Attempts to create personalities for computers, with the goal of attributing them with human characteristics, go way back to *Hal 9000* from *2001: A Space Odyssey* (as mentioned in *Chapter 1, Conversational UI is our Future*), *R2-D2* and *C-3PO* from *Star Wars*, and Pixar's *WALL-E*. Other more tragic robots include the *Terminator* or *Edward* from *Edward Scissorhands*.

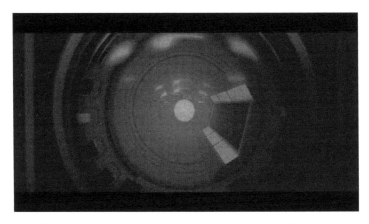

Figure 1: Hal 9000 (`https://www.imdb.com/title/tt0062622/videoplayer/vi1143322137`)

Figure 2: WALL-E; C-3PO and R2-D2 (image credit: `http://300-heroes.wikia.com/wiki/Wall-E`; `https://www.shutterstock.com/g/paulguzzo`)

These fictional robots were all given specific personalities and human characteristics, and, combined with their unique computer capabilities, a special *persona* was created. A persona is the aspect of someone's character that is presented to or perceived by others. The Latin term originated in the early 20th century and literally means a mask or a character played by an actor. In this case, the actors are the robots and they are given a mask or a unique character to present to us – the crowd.

According to Liraz Margalit, Ph.D., an analyst of online consumer behavior, when people interact with chatbots, their brain is led to believe that they are chatting with another human being. The reason is that bots create "a false mental perception of the interaction, encouraging the user to ascribe to the bot other human-like features they do not possess" (`https://www.psychologytoday.com/us/blog/behind-online-behavior/201607/the-psychology-chatbots`).

Whether you like it or not, your bot will be given a personality by your users, so you better design the personality you wish to give your bot to avoid that happening. The bot's personality is everything that your business or brand represents. It's the icon you choose for it, the language you give it, the voice it uses, and its style. Avoiding giving your bot a personality can "kill" your bot. Remember, your bot is replacing human-human interaction. Would you put a lifeless agent on the phone or in your store to welcome your clients?

Building personas

Beyond programming, AI development, and other technical concerns, drafting your bot's personality is by far one of the most difficult tasks when creating a good bot. Here are a few tips and ideas that you should take into consideration when "giving birth" to your bot.

Who can build it?

More specifically, who builds your bot's personality? We already talked about the different stakeholders of bot building. While the developers and programmers can figure out all the technical aspects, a different group of people can eventually design your bot's personality. They must understand the importance of personalities and be able to identify and connect the organization's users with the bot's persona. They should be able to understand the *story* behind the customer interaction and combine the right set of characteristics into one or more types of bot.

I call these people "masters of communications," but they are known as voice designers/creative writers. They can build a whole world from micro pieces of interactions that are represented as short messages, such as texting or short voice responses. Such people usually have a background in marketing. They know how to analyze different personas and how to build an interaction within limited spaces.

What's your bot's job description?

Have you ever written a job description? When we write a job description, we take into consideration multiple factors, including:

- Years of experience: Is it a beginner's job or are a certain number of years of experience required to best perform the daily tasks?

- Level/years of education: Should that person have a specific educational background? Is a high school diploma sufficient or should that person have a specific university degree?

- What are the personality characteristics we are looking for? Does the job require him/her to be tidy and organized, or maybe more creative and aspiring? Should they be friendly or rather serious and professional?

We basically have in mind a person who we think could perform the job in the best way, based on the requirements that we attach to the job. This is the same with your bot. First, think, if your bot was a person, who would it be? How would you like them to talk with your clients? What characteristics would they have?

By building a job description for your bot, you are also narrowing down its tasks and specialties. While we like to think we can build a "super-bot" that knows everything about everything, when we build a bot, just like when we recruit a person, that person – or bot – should have unique expertise. If a bot's goal is to provide you with fashion recommendations, then you can't really expect it to also help you with your annual tax filing.

The better your bot represents its job description, the better experience it will provide for its users, and the more it will be used. A major consideration for your bot's job description is also based on who its clients are.

Who are your bot's clients?

Your bot's clients are your clients. You know who they are, you know their personas, and you have hired people before to interact with them. Understanding your customers' personalities is crucial to building your bot's personality. Try to ask yourself:

1. Are you serving professional or leisure users? For example, are they looking for legal or romantic advice?

2. What is the age range of your users? Are they baby boomers or millennials?

3. What is the gender of your users? Are they young moms looking for breastfeeding consultations or men looking for advice on dating?

4. What is their geographic spread: where are they located in the world? Are they large-city users or small-town users?

5. What languages do they talk? Should your bot be multilingual?

6. What is the form of language they use?

   Do they write/interact in a formal or informal way?

   Do they use abbreviations or emojis?

   Do they prefer to interact using voice or text?

When you design a character that is a true match for your customer or customers (there will definitely be more than just one persona of your typical client), you must think how it will interact with a human – and what their expectations are – and then build that personality and those capabilities into your bot.

The best way to understand an interaction is to have a real person interacting with your clients within the scope of your bot's job description. Many companies use live-chat solutions and, by analyzing the conversations, you can learn a lot, both about your users' expectations, as well as how your agents respond. If this is not possible, try to mimic a dialogue that could potentially emerge between your clients and the bot and build a comparison of how your bot reacted versus how a person would. Have someone from outside of your development group interact with your bot and follow their conversation. You should focus on:

- The user's understanding of the bot's purpose: Does the user understand what the bot can help them with? Are the questions they ask aligned with the use cases you have built?

- The user's learning curve: How long does it take for the user to understand the scope of the bot?

- The bot's responses: The accuracy level of the responses. How well does the bot understand the request and how well does it provide the most accurate response?

- The bot's level of understanding when it can't help or when there is a problem: What are the responses to such a situation? Can the bot hand the conversation over to a real person? Can the bot instruct the user to ask the question differently? Can it identify at all that it can't help?

As we mentioned earlier, building a bot is an ongoing process. Once you put your bot out there, monitor your target audience and their requests. Maybe you missed someone when you identified your users' personalities, so make the relevant adjustments. Like any other development life cycle, your bot's personality will continue to grow and change with your clients.

Building your bot's personality

Once you have figured out your bot's job description and its target audience, you can start building its personality. The personality of your bot starts from its gender (if it has one at all), its voice and tone, its look, and of course its language and style.

Gender

It is questionable whether a bot should have a gender. If we agree that our bot is not presenting itself as a "real human," but rather declares that it is a bot - so basically a *machine* - from the very beginning of its interactions, then why should it have a gender?

I think there are multiple reasons for giving our bot a gender. First and foremost, and as claimed previously, just because we didn't give it a gender, it doesn't mean that it doesn't have one in the eyes of our users. As humans, we tend to use our imagination to build a description of the person we talk to on the other side. We base it on a person's voice, when we talk on the phone, or on their language and profession alism when we receive an email. An interaction with another person invokes us with the need to describe to ourselves who we "see" on the other side. A big part of this is also built on our expectations: who we expect to see on the other side, which goes back to the job description requirements. If we know our target audience, we know who they expect to see on the other side – so why not build that persona in the first place?

Another reason is trust. The gender transparency of a bot can also create trust among users. Continuing the preceding example, a young mom looking for breastfeeding advice may appreciate it coming from a "female" figure, rather than a "male" one. In this case, it is very easy to put it to the test and, after all, if this young mom had gone to a breastfeeding counsellor in person, the chances are that she would have ended up talking to a woman.

In many cases, it's not always clear what the bot's gender should be, so it is recommended to run some A/B testing and see the reaction and success rate of different gender bots. For example, if I interact with an investment adviser, should my bot be a male or female figure? This could even differ between users, age groups, and geographies. On the one hand, I would recommend using the gender figure that your users would expect to see if they met them in your store or branch. On the other hand, maybe this is a good time to break some biases (I'm not going to elaborate more on that but would recommend you give it some thought when building your bot).

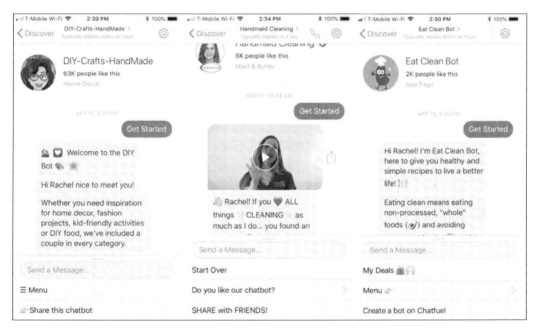

Figure 3: DIY-Crafts -Handmade: very female, using a housewife-type icon and emojis. This bot's looks and personality are definitely aimed at women; Handmaid Cleaning: very female-oriented – bias?; Eat Clean Bot: a non-gender bot (eggplant chef) that uses green, positive colors and a happy eggplant figure that symbolizes healthy food with a chef's hat. It is likely aimed at all genders.

Look and feel

Gender is only one component of the bot's look and feel. Whether it's a "man," a "woman," or something else (a robot or maybe an animal), your bot's personality can be reflected in so many ways through its color; accessories; clothing; hair color and style; eye shape, color and size; the existence or non-existence of wrinkles; and even facial expressions. What is it that you would like your bot to represent and how can it gain your users' trust with its appearance?

All those questions are easy (or at least easier) to answer once you have built your average customer's description and have analyzed the purpose of the bot. If there is more than one answer, put it to the test. For example, the Western Union bot has no gender, being represented by a very serious and trusty-looking logo, along with the use of positive pictures, as well as very thought-out language. The only problem is that, it failed to understand any request that wasn't part of the visual menu and repeatedly said, "I'm sorry, I don't understand." This of course has nothing to do with the bot's persona, but it's clear that just building a good persona is not enough.

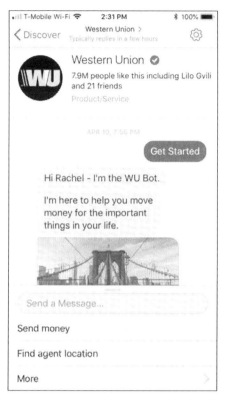

Figure 4: The Western Union bot has no gender

Voice and style

How does your bot "talk"? When I refer to the bot's voice, I refer to more than just its linguistic definition. Even a chatbot has a voice. A voice is the *style* and *tone* of the bot's conversation. It's the specific words that the bot uses when "talking" to the user. It's the small nuances, the emojis, the abbreviations, and even the energy it responds to the user with. These are all part of your brand's personality and they should be part of your bot's personality as well.

If your bot provides medical advice, it will use a formal style of interaction. It will have a relaxing and trustworthy tone and it should sound knowledgeable. It can even include links to other resources for further reading. However, if the purpose of your bot is to check whether your classmate likes you or not, or the chances of you marrying a famous actor, then your bot's voice should represent a teen-spirit attitude, with a friendly or even childish style. It may include emojis and funny GIFs to fit the mood.

By successfully identifying your users and use cases, you will probably succeed in giving your bot the right voice and tone too. Here, as well, the user must trust the bot and that it "knows" what to do. It must "speak" with the user in their language and style, and it should "talk" to him/her on their level. With every sentence you build into your bot's persona, you should ask yourself: Would the person behind my bot really say that? Is that the way they would phrase the sentence? Could they have said it differently or better?

Small talk = big success

We talked about narrowing down the field of expertise of the bot to help it to focus on specific use cases that it can be helpful with, however, chatter capabilities or small talk are a great way to break the ice and show your users that you understand them.

Small talk or chatter can either be related to the bot's scope or on general topics. In many cases, people "try" the bot to see how "human" it is. Small talk can also be a good response to an unidentified question. It's not a huge investment of time for you and it can make a huge difference. If you are using a tool that helps you to track the interactions, you can also see what people are actually saying and continue to build that database.

Chatter questions include questions such as:

♦ *How are you?*

♦ *Who are you?*

♦ *Are you a bot?*

♦ *Are you married?*

♦ *Who do you work for?*

♦ *Who pays you?*

♦ *What do you like to do/eat/drink?*

♦ *Do you have a boyfriend?*

♦ *Do you like me?*

Chatter responses are usually funny. They can also be informative, for example, the bot could answer, *I work for the NBA*, but it could also add a wink emoji and say, *I'm not getting paid so well*. Such a response is much better than saying, *I didn't get that.*

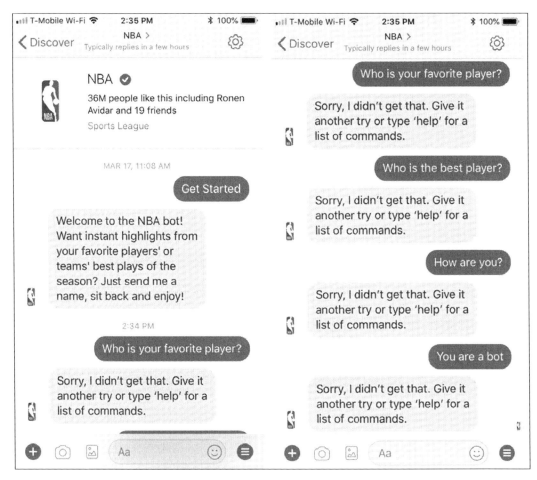

Figure 5: The NBA bot has no gender or personality and offers a limited experience when responding to questions that it would make sense to have an answer to, as well as to chatter questions. Those questions could have been easily answered with clever responses or funny ones. It feels like a real missed opportunity.

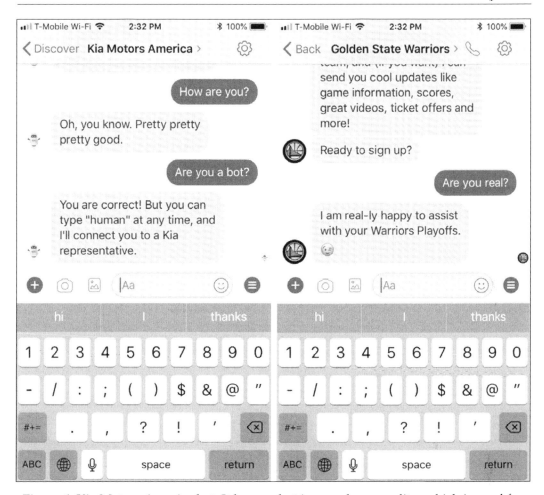

Figure 6: Kia Motors America bot: It has a robot icon and personality, which is good for providing general information but also for chatter discussions. The bot provides clever responses and has an understanding that I might need to talk to a real person, giving me information on how to do that; Golden State Warriors bot: It has a warrior icon, but no visual personality. The bot gives a nice response to the common test question *Are you real?* by sending a winking emoji icon. This is definitely a good icebreaker.

Figure 7: The Golden State Warriors bot reacts to me saying,
"It's my birthday" by sending Warrior-colored hearts – priceless!

Building multiple personas

We have mentioned the possibility that your bot is serving more than just one target audience. In many cases, you can't identify your users, but in cases where you can, it can be useful to assign different bots to different users. Why is this necessary? While the general business logic of the bot may not change, the conversational flow and the content or information provided may differ to the extreme.

Let's take, for example, a banking bot. It is clear that an interaction with a millennial will be different compared to an interaction with a retiree. Their topics of interest will be different since they have different needs and different prospects. This is why what the bot offers should also diverge. Also, the *way* that they interact, their *voice* and *style*, and choice of wording will be different. A human agent would be able to identify those differences immediately and react to them accordingly, and so should your bot.

While it makes everything a bit more complicated, being able to provide different bot personas for different users is a key factor in your bot's success, if you are providing services for a variety of customer types.

Methodologies for building your bot's personas

If you have some experience as a marketer, you probably know all that there is to know about how to build your customer's persona, and why it is so important. The goal is, of course, to know and understand your clients better, so that you can sell to them or serve them better. There are various methods for building a customer persona while collecting general information on the user, including geography, age, and profession, as well as more specific data that is related to the business itself. For example, if we were a big publisher, we would like to know whether our users are more interested in finance or fashion, to know where to invest our efforts.

Building a bot's persona is very similar, but with some differences. Austin Beer, a leader in UX design, developed a "Bot Persona Toolkit," which helps teams to create the personality of any bot they build. According to Beer, the fact that a group of people is gathered to build the persona and the bot, and not a single person, is the main difference between the classic customer persona and the bot's:

> *By using more collaborative and human-centric methods in our {bot R.B} design process, we are better able to create more empathetic experiences for our users (in other words, humans).*
>
> *—Austin Beer*

As part of the process, a group of people is required to answer five questions that will eventually shape the personality of the bot:

♦ My name is…

♦ My goal is…

♦ I do…

♦ I think…

♦ I feel…

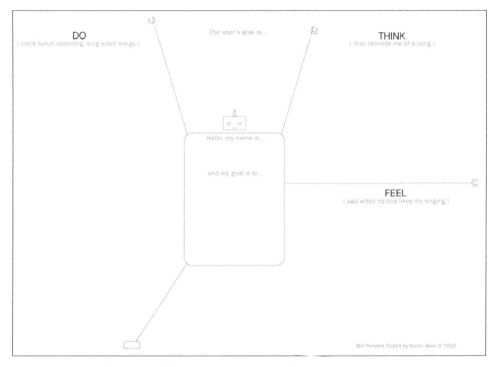

Figure 8: "The Bot Persona Toolkit" by Austin Beer

Using a similar method, Ari Zilnik, a UX designer, shared how he and his team built the personality of Emojibot, the host of Emoji Salad, a texting-based Pictionary-style game that uses emojis. Zilnik mentioned that they chose to give their bot the personality characteristics of celebrities and fictional figures. Working as a team, they were then able to find common characteristics that the different figures shared and connect them to the bot's personality on different scales.

Another interesting tool that can help you build the personality of your bot is actually a tool that was built to help humans to understand and identify their own personality's strengths (`https://www.16personalities.com/`). By answering a set of questions (it takes a around 10 minutes to complete), you get the results of your "personality test," stating what "type" of a person you are and a a more in-depth look at different scales of characteristics. I find this tool interesting to quickly test your bot's personality *after* you and your team have jointly built it based on the preceding requirements. You may find out at the end that your bot is not as compassionate as you hoped it would be!

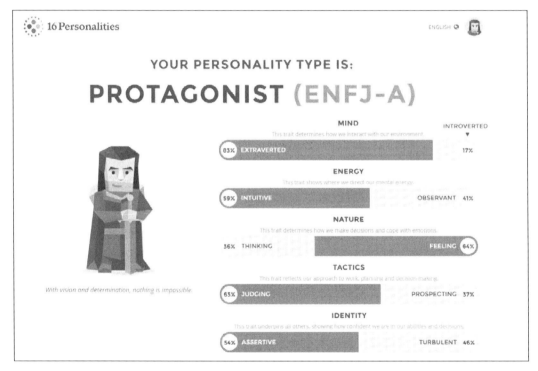

Figure 9: From 16 personalities, you can find out your bot's strengths

Summary

Our personality is what makes us unique as humans, so it only makes sense that when we try to mimic human-human interaction, we try to attach a unique personality to a bot. After overcoming some of the technical barriers of building bots, creating their personalities is probably one of the biggest challenges, and we are going to see very interesting developments in this space.

Building a bot's personality is a multifaceted process that includes many factors and parameters, such as the look and feel of the bot, language, style, tone, and voice. It requires us to start by identifying our clients' personas – their language, their age range, their style, and so on – in order to match them with the best "agent." We can end up with a serious, trusted bot, or a funny, silly one. In each case, the bot has to speak its users' "language."

Where possible, it is even recommended to create multiple personas for a bot, if you know in advance that you are targeting more than one type of person/client.

Looking at successful use cases, we can see that the process of building a bot's personality is performed better by a team, where each participant outlines their expectations and interpretation of the bot's goals and capabilities, and when brought together, a multifaceted automatic "agent" is born.

We also understand that bots are not (yet) human, but can be slightly better than a human in specific use cases, where we have narrowed down the fields of expertise. Your bot can grow and evolve, and you can help it to learn based on experiments and customers' real-time interactions. As noted pretty often in this book, building a bot is not a one-time process. It is a process of trial and error, and an ongoing learning cycle.

Lastly, as we learn the best ways to build our bot's personality, remember that we can all have some fun in the process. Give your bot a unique or funny angle, and help it to break the ice with your users, or at least put a smile on their face.

In the next chapter, we will dig into vertical-specific bots. We will discuss finance bots and travel bots, and look into their similarities and differences. Then, we will focus on a few examples and see what we can learn.

References

- For more famous robots: http://www.denofgeek.com/us/movies/19030/the-top-50-robots-and-ai-computers-in-the-movies

- https://en.oxforddictionaries.com/definition/personification

- *Persuasive Technology: Using Computers to Change What We Think and Do, B.J. Fogg, Morgan Kaufmann*

- https://chatbotsmagazine.com/designing-a-chatbots-personality-52dcf1f4df7d

- https://blog.marvelapp.com/guide-developing-bot-personalities/

- https://www.16personalities.com/free-personality-test

- https://www.theatlantic.com/technology/archive/2016/03/why-do-so-many-digital-assistants-have-feminine-names/475884/

- https://medium.com/the-charming-device/how-to-design-intelligence-3-ways-to-make-human-centered-bots-76c5ff7524df

8

A View into Vertical-Specific Bots – Financial Institutions

In previous chapters, we discussed the technology limitations and the lack of use of AI in creating "smart bots." While, on the one hand, many platforms today offer an easy and seamless bot-builder process, on the other hand, that same ease of development has introduced us to a huge number of low-functioning bots, which are no different than a simple web form or, a website's navigation tool.

We have learnt by now that bots are not necessarily cognitive and don't always involve AI in their processing, however, it is clear that this is where technology is heading. The possibility of learning from a user's behaviors and needs, and then reacting to and reimplementing those findings for other use cases is a crucial step in the evolution of bots. This is already being done today, to a certain extent, in some of the bots that we have explored in this book, however, as we have noticed, those processes are very siloed and vertical-oriented.

How can we expand this? How can we create a "mega brain" that will be able to correlate between different use cases, from various aspects? In the next two chapters, we will explore the question of bots' vertical functionality.

I chose to focus on two very interesting verticals: finance and travel, and in this chapter, we will see how some of the leading brands and institutions in these verticals have designed their solutions. While not necessarily different from other industries, the financial institution industry contains good, successful examples, following most of the best practices described in this book.

Before we dive deeper into the verticals-focused analysis, I want to discuss and question the need to build vertical-focused solutions. Does a bot's functionality truly differ from one vertical to another? Are there similarities that can be leveraged cross-vertical?

Can a banking bot become a travel bot?

I believe it can and will in the future. The concept of personal assistants, such as Siri and Alexa, will expand to allow cross-application interactions and recommendations. This is a highly complicated task, but by leveraging data, and with the right classifications using AI, this could be achieved.

In the meanwhile, we can leverage cross-bot and cross-vertical learning, mostly when approaching common use cases. Some of our banking use cases are similar to our travel/flight bot use cases and even insurance use cases or enterprise internal use cases, such as ticketing systems. For example, checking on the status of *<item>*.

For the banking use case, it could be:

What is the status of my loan application?

For the travel bot or flight status bot, it could be:

What is the status of my hotel reservation/flight?

For the enterprise ticketing or insurance use case, it could be:

What is the status of my ticket/my claim?

While the use cases are fairly different, the same form of interaction with the end user is required to create a successful conversation, assuming again that bots are replacing/imitating human behavior.

This is relevant for:

♦ The collection of samples (utterances) that are needed to support the NLU engine of the bot:

What is the status of my <item>?

What's the condition of my <item>?

Is there an update on the <item>'s status?

♦ The conversational flow itself. In the preceding example, in all use cases the bot's reply should probably be a form of asking for additional information, such as:

Can you please provide me with the number of your loan application/ hotel reservation/flight/ticket?

Other cross-vertical examples are password resetting and the cancellation of items. In the end, the response itself will be connected to the relevant API, which will extract the dynamic information for the user. When building the conversational flow, a lot can be learned from comparing one use case to another, and many of the improvements you make to a bot for a certain use case can be relevant to others.

For example, resetting your university user password is no different to resetting your online banking password – they only call at the back to different APIs, which require different information. The conversational flow remains the same, as in both cases the user will say, "I want to reset my password," or "I lost my password."

Financial institutions – use cases, implementation, and examples

Financial institutions are usually slow to adapt to new technologies due to security concerns, long decision-making processes, and, in many cases, a lack of knowledge and know-how. Often, by the time they adapt a new technology, it's no longer new or the implementation is so scarce that the solution remains useless. However, I chose to address the financial institution industry in this book, since I believe that conversational applications and conversational UI can be established more quickly in financial institutions (more quickly than other digital revolutions in the past), helping them and their customers to interact better. To understand this unique trend, there are three questions we need to ask: why, where, and what?

Why?

Banks are not new to voice. Phone banking and IVR systems have been an integral part of our banking experience for at least a decade. However, frustrating experiences with those very expensive solutions may have done more harm than good.

Seeking to improve their customer interactions, banks and other financial institutions welcome other methods of conversational communication. A solution that offers users a way to talk or text freely when they interact with a machine can be very charming for the bank and its users.

Where?

Everywhere: Financial institutions engage with their clients via combined online and offline endpoints. New conversational technologies offer them additional paths to connect with their clients via chat and voice, from Amazon Alexa, Google Home, chatbots and texting, even to an improved conversational phone experience.

What?

Financial institution use cases continue to grow and expand. Very similar to mobile, they started with non-personalized data, such as opening hours and address searches. However, lately, we have seen more and more financial institutions looking to take conversational interaction to the next level.

By offering access to our own data, chatbots and voicebots now provide financial information and advice, from checking on our account balance, to tracking our spending, and even completing a bill payment or money transfer. As a result, banks make themselves available to their users 24/7, with a very low overhead.

It is not only the customer support and self-service functions that are transitioning: it is also marketing and sales. This includes loan applications and new account generation, which are available to the user and actively encourage a conversation.

Financial institution chatbots

It was the large financial institutions that started and led the trend. They were then followed by some of the smaller ones. Some have created a framework and some have incorporated their conversational experiences into existing platforms.

Bank of America

Erica is an in-app chat and voicebot that provides Bank of America's members with information on their account balances and transactions, but also offers the capability to transfer money and pay bills. It is expected to provide financial recommendations using more AI capabilities as it continues to grow.

Erica was in development for almost 12 months and the team included more than 100 developers and designers. It is currently not available on third-party devices, such as Amazon Alexa or Google Home, or through texting, and it supports only English.

The adoption among the bank's users was amazing: in less than three months, one million members were already taking advantage of the virtual assistant on the app, according to the bank's officials. The reasons were that it:

♦ Fulfilled a need

♦ Used a good conversational design

Erica's personality and its connection to the bank are strongly presented in its name am*ERICA*, as a shorter version of *America*, with a feminine connection. It has no "face," as it is represented by the bank's logo and the entire interface continues the brand's overall offline and online design pattern. As discussed in previous chapters, this may have an influence on the way that people trust and connect with the bot.

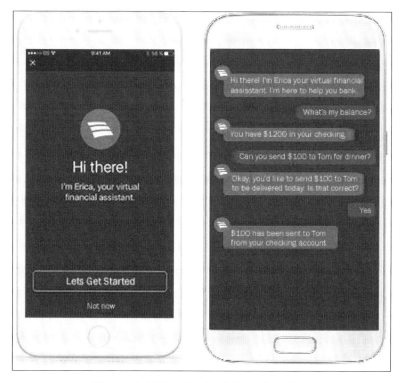

Figure 1: Erica, Bank of America's bot

The conversational interface offers a short, focused interaction between the end user and the virtual banker. The scope of interaction (number of use cases) is broad and includes general questions, as well as account-related information. Using AI, Erica is able to provide financial advice and therefore can become more active in the user's banking experience and account management.

Interactions are quick and short and is fulfill the need for immediate, accessible banking advice.

The bot's persona is lacking visuality and this might be something that will change over time, especially as other companies adopt a unique figure that the end user can connect with.

Wells Fargo

The Wells Fargo banking assistant originally leveraged the FB Messenger platform to interact with its clients. It offered account balance data, transaction insights, and other general services.

Similar to Erica, Wells Fargo kept its assistant's persona very natural, simply leveraging the Wells Fargo logo as an icon. In this case, the name that was given to it, Wells Fargo Banking Assistant, represented its functionality and not a unique figure.

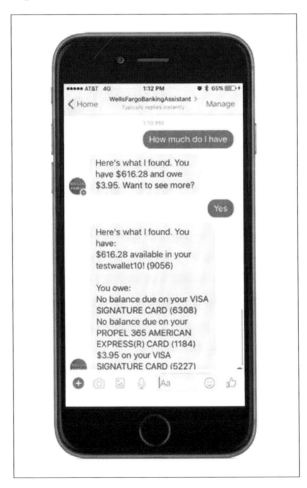

Figure 2: The Wells Fargo FB Messenger bot – a strategy change

The Wells Fargo FB bot no longer exists. In a message reply sent to me a few hours after I tried to access it, I was informed that, due to security reasons, account information is no longer available on social media (probably due to the latest FB data scandal).

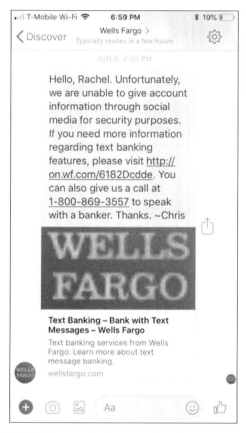

Figure 3: Wells Fargo shifting its banking conversational
strategy to other channels outside of FB

The bank does offer a texting solution as a conversational experience. This texting bot, however, includes no branding or personality and it requires pre-registration on the bank's website or via mobile.

As part of the pre-registration, only specific pre-defined options are enabled and the user is asked to use code-based commands, instead of free-speech conversational UX (see the following screenshot):

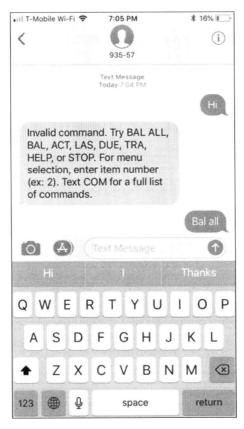

Figure 4: The Wells Fargo texting solution – can we go back to that?

UI and UX best practices

Looking at some the industry leaders in the financial vertical, we can learn from and mimic some best practices. I've picked a few of those in the following sections.

Wells Fargo

Not many best practices are to be found in the Wells Fargo example, but we have the possibility of learning from its mistakes.

Wells Fargo, as opposed to Bank of America, chose to enable its bot interaction via FB Messenger, which, as mentioned, may have been the wrong decision due to security reasons. While the FB bot originally had all the relevant functionalities of a virtual banker, its functionality and scope were limited to non-personal data, and the bot is not accessible at all now.

I do expect to see Wells Fargo adopting its own chatbot strategy very soon (within its app/website) in a secure and safe environment for its clients. For now, conversational interactions, in their modern form, are not available for Wells Fargo clients. This is also a reason to make the effort to work multi-channel and not put all of your eggs in one single basket.

Capital One

Eno ("one" spelt backwards) is a texting solution that allows customers to receive information on their accounts, as well as pay their credit card bill. Different from the other examples, Eno is gender-neutral and has a different persona to the classic Capital One branding. It carries the same colors on the app.

Eno's persona is much more casual and light. It responds to emojis and abbreviations and it feels as if it is targeting a millennial user experience. Capital One also insisted on providing Eno outside of the app, to avoid forcing its clients to download the app in order to leverage their intelligent assistant capabilities. This represents a shift from mobile to conversational. In many ways, this makes total sense, offering the user another communication path outside the mobile app?

Capital One uses a texting platform to bring a new wave of conversational experience to its users. Together with its broad functionality, I would conclude that this is definitely today's most advanced financial institution chat experience.

Eno was introduced to the public after Capital One's Alexa skill (on which I will elaborate in the following section).

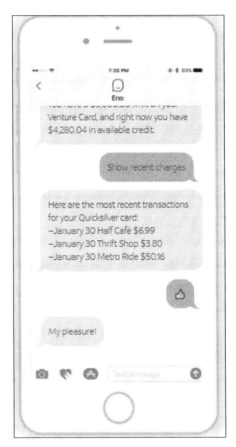

Figure 5: Eno is one very good example to learn from – it feels like chatting with a person

It is clear that Eno's designers have put a lot of effort into building its character, which has led to the "birth" of a non-gender – but still very human – bot offering a unique customer experience. The bot offers a great combination of meaningful and broad functionality, together with a multi-faceted personality that is very easy and intriguing to connect with.

Capital One was the first to invest in voice conversational UI, which I believe had a lot of influence on its chat conversational UI. Being able to design a visual-free conversation challenges voice designers to create a much more complex and flawless communication. Conversation is focused and short, but it has the ability to react to many branches when needed.

Other financial institution chatbots, which include mostly general queries and customer support, are the Swedish bank SEB's assistant Aida, the Hong Kong HSBC assistant Amy, and some others. Interestingly enough, they all have women's names and in the latter examples, they also have a feminine appearance (see the following screenshots). The reason for this is gender stereotypes. We are used to having women as assistants and formal welcoming figures.

Here, as well, we can see that banks are still being very cautious about providing personal information to their users and the customer is also advised to avoid providing personal information. The design, however, is more of a web design and less of a conversational one.

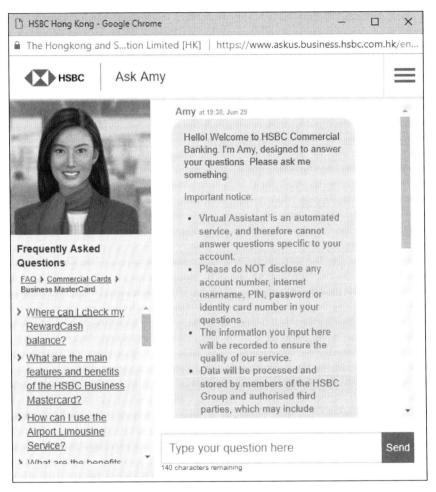

Figure 6: Amy, the HSBC virtual assistant

Financial institution voice-enabled conversational bots

Financial institutions have been slower at adapting third-party conversational devices. Two very innovative companies in the US to have done that are Capital One and GEICO, the auto insurance company.

Capital One

We already saw Capital One's innovative thinking in its unique texting solution. However, Capital One's innovation started way back when it was the first to introduce an Amazon Alexa skill to its members.

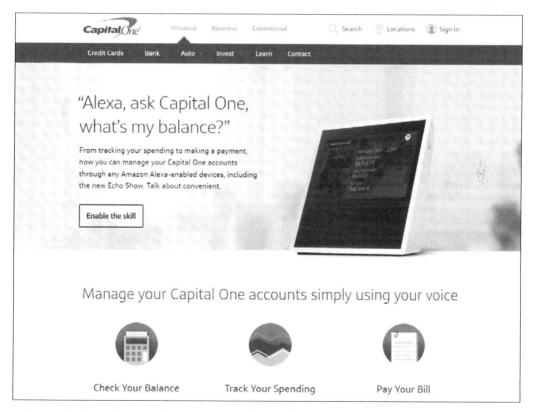

Figure 7: From Capital One's website: Alexa's first financial skill was for Capital One

In March 2016, Capital One became the first company to offer its customers a way to interact with their financial accounts through Amazon Alexa devices. The skill started by offering customers access to real-time data from their accounts and has gradually grown to enable bill payments.

On the Amazon Developer site, there is a full description of the use case (`https://developer.amazon.com/blogs/alexa/post/c70e3a9b-405c-4fe1-bc20-bc0519d48c97/the-story-of-the-capital-one-alexa-skill`) and it's interesting to see how the skill has evolved over time. On top of the different interactions, Capital One also continued to leverage Amazon's new devices' capabilities, including the screen-enabled device – Echo Show.

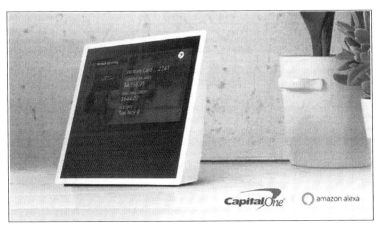

Figure 8: From Capital One's website: Echo Show supports a wide
range of functionalities, from simple to complex use cases

As a pioneer in this market, together with the Amazon Alexa team, Capital One has paved the way to voice-enabled conversational banking, encouraging other institutions to take this path. Also, in terms of security, Capital One and the Alexa team have incorporated a unique mechanism that enables strict security protocols and flows, without harming the user experience.

By enabling cross-channel conversational solutions through text and voice, Capital One has been leading the conversational revolution in the banking world. Whether users prefer to talk or text, Capital One offers a true cross-platform conversational experience and a new standard in the industry.

On both channels, Capital One provides fresh conversational interaction that follows the goals of a chatbot to replace human interaction. The conversation is short and precise, on both text and voice. As mentioned previously, the fact that Capital One started with voice gave it some advantage when its texting solution was built, making the two very similar.

Capital One's Alexa and Eno's personas are a bit different. Eno's character is younger and lighter, while Alexa is more moderate. This might be because it's more difficult to create a genderless voice assistant and therefore the Alexa skill, presenting a feminine character, wasn't given the same characteristics.

On the UX side, both solutions offer short and focused interactions that are very conversational in their manner. In both examples, the bots offer discovery information as to what else can be asked and what is new with their capabilities.

Capital One has yet to release a Google Home action, which remains a mystery to many users. It will definitely be very interesting to follow the next releases coming from Capital One over the next 12 months.

GEICO

A unique persona use case in voice was introduced by the insurance company GEICO, as we described in *Chapter 3*, *Building a Killer Conversational App*. In this specific use case, GEICO didn't create a new persona for its Alexa skill (and thereafter its Google Home action), but rather connected it to its brand mascot – Gecko.

Gecko is the longest-running mascot, appearing in more than 150 commercials as of 2017. It was first introduced in 1999 and its personality was built and modified over the years in GEICO's commercials and advertising campaigns. It started as a sophisticated figure, but over the years it has turned more and more into a "boy next door" persona.

However, it is Gecko's voice that has made GEICO's voice experience so different. Gecko speaks with a distinguished British accent (currently recorded by Jake Wood, a British actor), which is easily identified thanks to the company's TV and radio commercials (GEICO counts as one of the largest spenders on commercials: in 2016, it was the top spending brand in the United States `https://en.wikipedia.org/wiki/GEICO_advertising_campaigns#The_Gecko`).

While both Alexa and Google Home have a few voice options to choose from, GEICO found a very interesting way to combine Gecko's voice with those devices' experience.

Figure 9: GEICO's voice experience – unique and surprising
(https://www.ispot.tv/ad/7tDc/geico-arrrrrrr)

As we explained briefly in *Chapter 3, Building a Killer Conversational App*, when activating the Alexa skill or the Google action, the interaction starts with a few lines of introduction to the application, using a recording of Gecko's voice. It begins by welcoming the user to the app and letting them know what they can achieve by interacting with it. It ends by asking the user what they would like to do next. When the user answers, Gecko hands over the conversation to the Alexa/Google voices. When the user exits, Gecko's voice kicks in with a farewell message.

The skill and the action offer balance information, road side assistance, and bill payment. While still only offering a few limited use cases, GEICO started with more complex use cases, likely paying attention to solving specific needs. Like other companies, GEICO will probably continue to add more functionalities as customers adopt new voice-enabled devices.

Conversations are kept focused and short, and the interactions are fluent and natural. The user is given some information on what they can use the skill or action for (the use cases covered) and can navigate through the different steps at will (contextual conversation).

Figure 10: Gecko using Alexa

Similar to Capital One, after releasing its Alexa skill, GEICO also introduced an intelligent assistant named Kate. Kate is an in-app voice and chat assistant that aims to provide answers to general questions, as well as personal information for very similar use cases to GEICO's skill and action.

Kate doesn't hold Gecko's persona. Although the bot was given a feminine name, Kate is represented by a colorful variation of the company's icon and not a specific character.

Figure 11: Kate, GEICO's chatbot

Similar to Capital One, GEICO also started rather early with voice and, as such, has had the time to improve and grow its use cases and functionality over time. The fact that there are multiple assistants on different platforms, with different offerings, may become confusing for clients, but this can be solved through consolidation across the different channels.

GEICO's Alexa and Google personas using Gecko are a good example of personalization and branding (again, still lacking on some of the conversational channels). This is the beginning of a new trend and a need that we will see in the market for personalized voice interactions, which will become the next challenge for voice, especially for dynamic interactions.

Summary

Conversational chat and voice interactions are starting to play a part in our everyday lives. Use cases from different industries resemble each other in their flow and business logic, and I believe that we can agree that, to some extent, our experience of building a banking bot can serve us when building a travel bot and many other vertical-related bots.

In this chapter, we learned that focusing on the right use cases, and combining them with a conversational user experience, is crucial for the success of a chatbot or voicebot. Looking into the various implementation methods in the financial sector, we also saw that the deployment focus still circles around the in-app experience, and not necessarily on leveraging external devices and mediums.

Larger companies continue to invest many resources and efforts into developing and bringing proprietary AI-conversational solutions to the market. The focus is on *self-learning* solutions that *understand* users and react to them in the same way as a human agent.

The goal, as always, is convenience for the client and long-term cost reduction for the company. However, here, we are also witnessing a major shift. Companies embrace texting platforms, and even Alexa and Google Home solutions, while trying to adapt to consumers' behavior, instead of forcing users to use a specific method to consume information. While this can be tricky, as we saw in the Wells Fargo FB example, especially due to the lack of transparency with security and data concerns, it also gives smaller brands a new opportunity to introduce such advanced solutions to their clients.

Brands and financial institutions are still experimenting with and exploring the use cases and the personas of their automated conversational applications. While Bank of America keeps a very conservative view, other companies, such as Capital One, are trying to connect their conversational innovation with a fresher look, reacting to millennial trends.

Voice brings a whole new challenge with it. The lack of graphic UI and UX makes it more difficult to create a unique persona and experience. GEICO found a creative way to bring something different into its Alexa skills and Google Home actions, while others are focusing mostly on the experience, use cases, and efficiency.

While being slower in adapting to new technologies as a sector, larger financial institutions also have huge budgets which allow them to experiment and test different solutions ahead of the market. Specifically, in the voice market in the US, financial institutions have been pioneers and surprised us with their innovative approaches. I anticipate seeing much more innovation coming from this industry, paving the way for others.

In the next chapter, we will take a look at bots in the travel and E-Commerce industries.

References

♦ Chatbots in financial institutions: `https://thefinancialbrand.com/71251/chatbots-banking-trends-ai-cx/`

♦ Bank of America's Erica passes 1 million users: `https://www.americanbanker.com/news/mad-about-erica-why-a-million-people-use-bank-of-americas-chatbot`

- Conversational applications replace traditional voice banking: `https://conversation.one/2018/06/27/how-conversational-applications-replace-traditional-phone-banking-and-ivrs/#more-2154`

- A Capital One Alexa skill use case on Amazon Developer: `https://developer.amazon.com/blogs/alexa/post/c70e3a9b-405c-4fe1-bc20-bc0519d48c97/the-story-of-the-capital-one-alexa-skill`

- Geico's advertising campaigns: `https://en.wikipedia.org/wiki/GEICO_advertising_campaigns#The_Gecko`

- `https://www.geico.com/more/geico-community/commercials/gecko-journey-across-america/`

9

TRAVEL AND E-COMMERCE BOTS – USE CASES AND IMPLEMENTATION

Travel and e-commerce are two great examples of industries implenting bots. Buying online or reserving our next flight or hotel is something we do very casually nowadays, via our computers and, increasingly, on our mobile phones.

I remember the first time I booked a flight on my mobile phone. It felt so strange and exciting to actually be able to complete such a complex task – end-to-end – using only my smartphone.

According to an Adobe research study, mobile holiday shopping in 2017 surpassed desktop (in the months of November and December, the amount in dollars from desktop was still higher, though, and accounted for 66% compared to 34% from mobile, which showed a 6% increase from 2016 `https://techcrunch.com/2017/11/02/mobile-holiday-shopping-visits-in-u-s-will-surpass-desktop-for-first-time/`). Shopping online, whether using desktop or mobile, is natural for us and has become so easy.

It only made sense that the two industries would identify the potential of bots and react to it quickly. However, some of the advantages that these industries had when moving online became a disadvantage when transitioning to bots.

In this chapter, we will discuss the challenges of travel and e-commerce bots, explore successful and less successful use cases, and consider how these industries can improve their user's bot experience. We will start with the two main challenges that both industries face and then we will take an in-depth look at the examples.

Travel and E-Commerce challenges

The travel and e-commerce industries have two common challenges that make it very difficult for any new solution to have an immediate impact:

♦ Current solutions are very advanced

♦ The discovery challenge

I consulted some of my colleagues before writing this chapter and asked them to refer me to the best bot – whether voice or chat – that they could recommend in these industries. The recommendations I received for the travel industry weren't necessarily for good companies, but rather for large companies that have already implemented a bot solution. In the e-commerce category, Amazon and Google were recommended many times. We all agreed that there isn't yet a bot that truly makes a difference in the industry and that we still have a long way to go. But why is that?

Can you compete with something that is already successful?

The first challenge is the fact that today's digital solutions are good enough, if not very good, and are very difficult to compete with. e-commerce sites and mobile apps, as well as travel apps and even hotel websites, are efficient, quick, and comfortable. Digital solutions in these industries have caused disruption and a change in our behavior. What started as a complementary service ended up being a complete solution of its own.

Digital solutions replaced the "physical" interactions in these industries because they offered a *different* and *better* experience, not because they were able to duplicate an existing one.

In order for chatbots and voicebots to be able to dominate these industries, they also need to offer a *different* and *better* experience than current digital solutions. They must provide the end user with more *added value*. If the end user can reach the same results using a bot or a website, then the bot has no added value. Finding the secret sauce of bots for travel and e-commerce is a great industry challenge.

Let's go back to the purpose of why we are building or using a bot. It needs to:

♦ Make interactions simple, seamless, and efficient for the end user

♦ Enable the business to provide a better service, at scale

♦ Have lower costs

If a bot does not accomplish these "three sacred" parameters, then it will probably never replace today's existing solutions.

The vast majority of today's bots (some were presented in earlier chapters of the book) merely provide a unique experience or information. At best, they offer the same value as a website/mobile browsing, and in other less successful examples, they end up referring the user back to the website to get answers. Were you ever referred back to a human agent when you simply searched for flights on KAYAK? If we fall back to the old paradigm, it means that the new one is just not strong enough.

Another important point to note is that most bots are only available as FB bots and are not on the business' website. This is in order to allow the end user to gain access to the business from the endpoints that they use the most – and no doubt social media is one of them. However, a good bot will help users to reduce their navigation efforts and deliver a response they are looking for on a website too, not just on other platforms. Only when businesses trust their bots enough to put them on their website will we see a true shift of paradigm.

With that said, it doesn't mean that automatic interactions will not replace today's digital solutions. I actually believe they will. They will just have to offer something much better than what we commonly see today in order to dominate. They will have to prove their added value and prove their ROI.

We have been investing in desktop and mobile apps for over two decades so far, and human behavior has been analyzed and researched so much that those solutions have excelled in the user interface and experience that they offer, and that makes them very hard to compete with.

Bots are still in their early days and we haven't yet had the number of years invested in them that other digital solutions have. It will take some time to figure out the secret sauce(s) and to implement them.

One of them will be voice. I believe that voice will have a much bigger influence on the design of bots and automatic interactions, and on making them the dominant solutions, which leads me to the next challenge: discovery and data presentation.

How do chatbots and voicebots manage data presentation?

This is with no doubt the number one challenge for chatbots, and even more so for voicebots. Whereas the web revolution exposed us to an infinite amount of data, the goal of chatbots and voicebots is to screen this data for us and and provide us with a short and focused response. The question, of course, is: is it at all possible to deliver such an experience in the travel and e-commerce industries?

In both cases, there are some clear use cases, where short, focused solutions make sense. For travel, for example, it would make sense to ask a question like:

Is my flight on time?

We can expect a short answer of "yes" or "no" and, if not, for the bot to provide us with the new flight times. The same is true with shopping. The user can ask questions about their order. For example:

Was my order shipped?

Or:

What's in my shopping cart?

The bot will easily be able to provide a response: "Yes, your order was shipped and is expected to arrive on...," or "You have milk and bread in your shopping cart; would you like to checkout?"

There are probably a couple of dozens of such examples that would make sense for short chat/voice interactions. However, the real challenge is in the discovery mode.

Discovery means the search for data. How can we make a data search short, focused, and user-friendly when we shop or when we book a flight? The amount of data that is available to us today is sometimes endless, and we can browse through it for as long as we wish. How can we bring this experience to chat or voice? Well, we don't: we build a better one.

Defining a new data discovery model

As you may recall, chatbots and voice-enabled bots are replacing our interaction with humans, not with websites or mobile apps. Therefore, instead of trying to mimic the current digital experience, we will go back in time to mimic interactions with human agents.

Web and mobile search provided us with limitless results. We were no longer dependent on the travel agent or the salesperson in the store – we could see it all and make our own analysis of what we would like to choose and eventually purchase. However, the amount of data was overwhelming.

To narrow down the options, filters were introduced. When we look look just for a t-shirt – we can now filter our search based on size, color, brand, and other factors. It's the same when we look for flights or vacations: we can filter the data based on arrival and departure dates, locations, airlines, and so on. However, even with filtering options, we are still exposed to hundreds, if not thousands, of results whenever we search for a hotel on `booking.com` or whenever we look for something on `amazon.com`. They are presented to us according to accuracy level, but even if we stick just to the two first pages, we end up with at least 15-40 results. Is this data valuable to us?

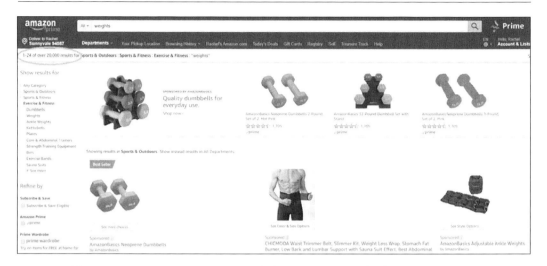

Figure 1: `amazon.com`: A search for weights resulted in 20,000 items.
Does this data help me?

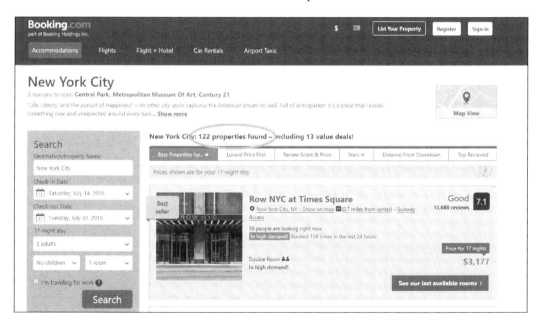

Figure 2: `booking.com`: 122 options were found for my trip
to New York – do I really need them all?

The real question is: even if this data is valuable, how can it be presented to us if we use a chat or texting solution, or if we just interact using voice? The answer to this is probably the first ingredient in our "secret sauce" discovery process for chatbots for travel and other industries.

Since we can agree that offering 20,000 options when I ask to buy weights doesn't really help me on existing digital channels, we understand that there is no reason that bots will act in the same way. A bot's mission is to do the exact opposite for us – its role is to crawl through all this big data and reply to us with the one-to-three best available options. Using AI and a smart conversational flow, bots will become our smart assistants, whom we will trust to pick up only the best results for us.

Data should be minimized and presented/given to us using voice in small chunks. We will be presented only with the best results for us and this will be supported by an advanced contextual interaction between us and the bot.

The experience must mimic our travel agent interaction, but it will be backed by the power and strength of what has been learned over the years by implementing web and mobile digital experiences.

Search engines will also have to improve, in order to enable the effectivity of bots. Filtering options and contextuality will become even more important. It's not only a dress I'm looking for: it's a dress for a cocktail event, for example.

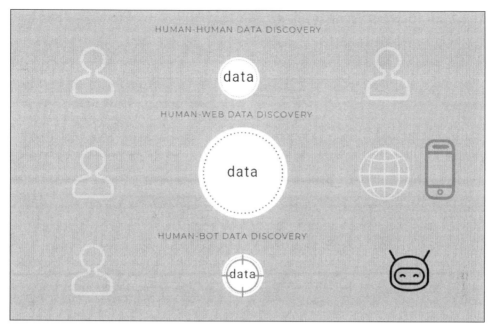

Figure 3: The evolution of data discovery – smart and focused

Use cases and recommendations

In this section, we will focus mostly on data discovery use cases and less on informative use cases, where a bot provides only a website's data.

Travel

The travel industry is one of the most progressive when it comes to digital solutions. Although still in the early phases, some of the large brands have already incorporated conversational UI and UX, supporting both voice and text.

As I was writing this chapter, I was referred to various companies offering virtual concierge services (Gooster, Ivy by Go Moment, Volara, and so on), which interact with guests mostly via texting or FB (Volara is supporting Amazon Alexa). The services check with guests whether their stay was good and provide answers to general concierge questions. I tested some, read about others, and also held some discussions with those companies' founders.

My conclusion was that those solutions offer very important information, which can prevent many of the questions asked at the front desk, and probably ease the guest's stay. However, they are all still very preliminary and deal with the simpler use cases.

To understand the discovery challenge, I chose to take a look at KAYAK, which offers both chat and voice solutions, from which we can learn a lot.

KAYAK

My use case on KAYAK was searching for a flight from San Francisco to New York. The flow was great and the bot was able to figure out the information that I provided very well.

As a FB Messenger bot, it combines both free-text and quick buttons. In some cases, I could use both and in some only the quick buttons.

When starting the flow of conversation with the bot, it let me know the use cases that it covers (find hotel, flight, or just things to do), and it also pointed me to some general question examples, such as "what's the best time to fly?" and even offered help planning a trip, which are all relatively complex use cases.

What went well and what didn't?

1. **Abbreviation support**: The bot was able to understand abbreviations when I replied "SF" to the question of where I was flying from (see the following screenshot):

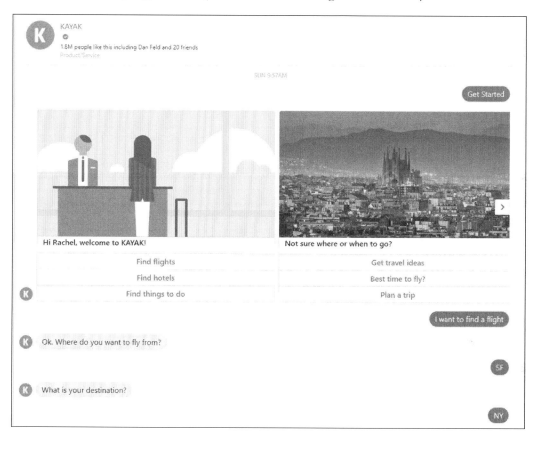

Figure 5: For some reason, when I entered "NY", the bot wasn't sure of my request and offered me two other options, which were very far from my request

2. **Understanding dates**: When asked when I wished to fly, I replied, "Tomorrow." For the question of when I wished to return, I replied, "Next Wednesday." The system was able to pick up the date and time and translate them, in order to provide me with the relevant itinerary. I didn't need to provide the specific dates (I could have, of course, if I'd wanted to) so it felt as if a real human was doing the calculations for me.

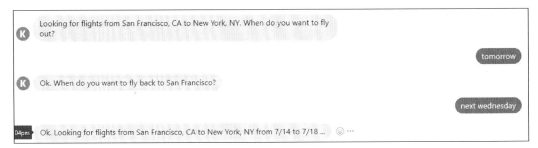

Figure 6: It calculated the dates for me and summarized my flight details perfectly:
I wanted to fly from San Francisco to New York, departing on July 14th and
returning on the 18th

3. **Results**: This is unfortunately where the bot failed to help me and provide me with the accurate, focused data I needed in order to complete the process. Instead of offering me the best flights, I received 1,062 options to choose from (see the following screenshot). This was only for one direction.

Figure 7: Do we need all of this data? Can we handle it all?

What could KAYAK do to improve this experience? It should ask for more information that would help it to narrow down the options, such as:

- "Would you like to depart early or late?"
- "Is there a specific airport you'd like to arrive to in NY?"
- "Are you looking for a non-stop flight?"
- "Is there a budget we should take into consideration?"

Questions like this can help a company to provide a more accurate and effective response for the end user. Think again about the travel agent you are replacing – can you imagine them telling you that they found more than 1,000 flights that might suit your needs?

4. **Selection**: I don't think I would have continued this interaction in real life, but for the purpose of the demo I continued my conversation and tried to see whether the bot could help me narrow down the results. I asked only for the cheapest ones and then decided to pick the United flight.

The bot didn't react to my questions, although the texting option was available. If we don't want to enable a texting option, we should disable it, otherwise the end user might think that there is something wrong in the process. I continued and clicked on one of the flights, just to discover that I also needed to browse through over 1,000 return flights...

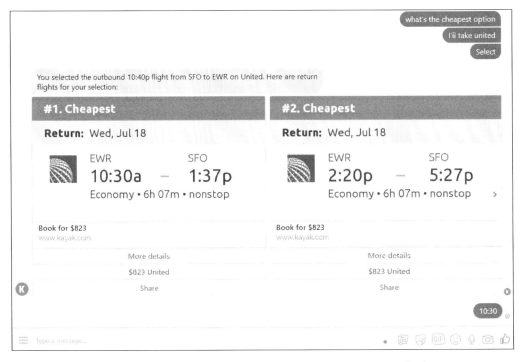

Figure 8: I needed to browse through over 1,000 return flights

5. **Complete the order**: I wasn't able to complete the booking for the flight and I was redirected to the website to continue the purchase there. It would have been very interesting if I could have completed the purchase while talking with the bot, and I believe that this is something that we will see in the future.

KAYAK on Alexa

I can't show my experience on Amazon Alexa, however, the flow using KAYAK on Alexa was very seamless and positive.

The skill offers information on flights, hotels, and cars. When I searched for hotels, I was also offered the option to book one for the number of nights I needed. In the two use cases (hotel search and flight search), the system handled content discovery very well, and the skill helped me by narrowing down the information in such a way that I could make a choice at the end.

Here is a more detailed analysis of the two use cases.

Hotel search

When I asked for hotels in New York, Alexa provided me with a limited number of options (three options). This is a perfect example of how data discovery on voice becomes focused and targeted, and I hope to see this shift in textual chatbot solutions.

I wasn't, however, able to add more search parameters and narrow my search. The three options that I received were quite expensive for my budget (ranging from $350 to $1,000 per night) but I wasn't able to ask for a cheaper place or to change the location.

Once this functionality becomes available, it will not only make the experience better, but it will also really enable people to complete a booking on Alexa.

A quick note about the Echo Show experience: I talked with KAYAK over Echo Show, which, as we covered in *Chapter 4, Designing for Amazon Alexa and Google Home* is Amazon's screen device and offers the additional visual value of the skill. It provided general topic-related images of hotel rooms and airplanes, and specific pictures of the hotels that it offered to book. Echo Show also supported the verbal interaction with additional data. For example, when it asked, *How long will you stay in the hotel?* Echo Show's screen showed *how many nights will you stay?*.

Flight search

My flight search using KAYAK was also very focused and targeted. After providing dates and destinations, Alexa returned with two options: the cheapest non-stop flight and the cheapest flight with one stop. When using voice, it is obvious for everyone that giving over 1000 options doesn't make sense. KAYAK automatically filtered the most popular parameters for me – which is a great way to solve the data discovery challenge.

Here, as well, we experience the narrowing down of options to choose from, which is exactly what we need when we voice or chat search.

I assume KAYAK is still developing its Alexa skill, since I wasn't able to continue the filtering process and to ask for a different time, airline, or airport. I believe that this will become available soon and that this is just the beginning of KAYAK's conversational offering for its clients.

E-Commerce

The potential for e-commerce and chatbots is huge as, from sales to support, there is so much that can be done. In previous chapters, we gave some examples of chatbot shopping experiences, which weren't very successful in most cases. I decided to include eBay's ShopBot example here, since it is different in terms of what it offers and its conversational design.

eBay

eBay's ShopBot, as its name implies, is there to encourage the user to shop by providing them with the best consultancy on any product they are interested in. The overall experience is very positive and it's even fun and amusing. The bot's persona is well thought out and the interaction feels very human. Different from other examples we've seen, it also helps you to complete a purchase at the end. It really felt as if I was talking to a knowledgeable human agent.

What went well and what didn't?

1. **Thought out and structured, yet flexible**: Getting started on a bot can be overwhelming, so the eBay bot provides some of its own suggestions. They are not the general bot capabilities menu suggestions. I was offered items relevant for the season.

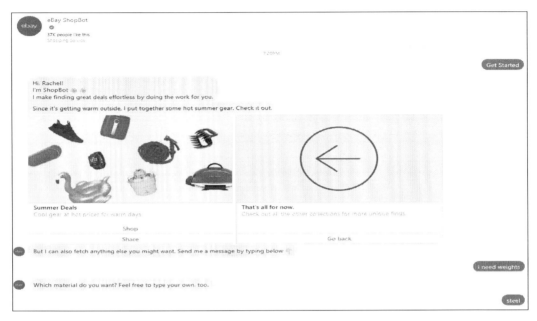

Figure 9: The bot makes it clear to the user that these are just suggestions and that the user can also lead the conversation in a different direction

2. **Filtering and narrowing down the options**: Once the user decides what they are interested in, the bot starts with a series of questions, with the aim of narrowing down the information and providing better data discovery. I was looking for weights and the bot asked me to choose the material of the weights that I wanted.

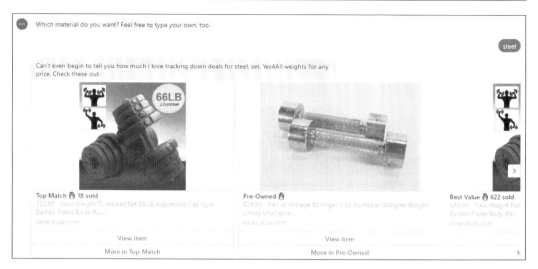

Figure 10: With this basic filtering, the bot is already providing a few options
that might be relevant for me and puts them into known categories, such as "best value",
"pre-owned", or "top match". While there is still a scrolling option to move right
and left for more results, the total amount of options is kept to six.

3. **Persona and communication**: The interaction with the bot is amusing and intuitive. It replies with full sentences that are more than just information or instructions. An example can be seen in the preceding screenshot: after running through the first filtering flow, the bot concludes the search by saying, *Can't even begin to tell you how much I love tracking down deals...*

4. The bot is also very instructive and informative: it lets me know that I can type text or click on the item for more information and, even in the preceding sentence, it reminds me that it can find the best deals for me.

5. **Continuous filtering**: What eBay did here is great. Instead of tiring people with 10 filtering questions at the beginning of the conversation, it created an ongoing filtering process, where, in between, the user gets some recommended suggestions based on the information already collected.

After asking me about the material of the weights, the bot continued to narrow down the options by asking me for the amount of money I planned to spend. With this information, I was exposed to even more focused search results.

Figure 11: Here, again, the process is not done and another filtering option is being offered – for what activity will you use the weights? Immediately after I provide the answer, the bot filters the information for me again.

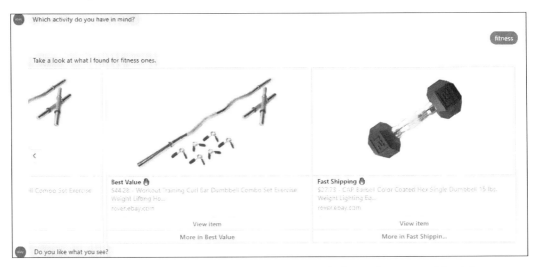

Figure 12: The bot continues the interaction with the end user until he/she is satisfied – the eBay ShopBot replaces the human reps at the store.

6. **Completing a purchase**: A couple of small things didn't go so well when I tried to complete the purchase. When I picked an item and shared the information with the bot, it understood my request and instructed me to click on the item I liked to learn more. When I asked if I could purchase it, I received a fallback answer that was out of context. It would have been much better if the bot had just directed me to click again on the item if I wished to purchase it (see the following screenshot).

Figure 13: The textual conversational interaction ends
and the user can now only click to view the item.

When I finally clicked on the item I wished to purchase, a small window opened (although I was on a desktop) where I could complete the purchase. I was sent back to the web experience.

It would have been nice if the purchase was completed as part of the interaction with the bot. However, it might be that this is done for security reasons (to avoid sending credit card details over FB) and therefore a web view is required. In this case, eBay should have paid attention to the size of the web view screen and probably also allowed me to sign in to my account, so I didn't have to provide my details and mailing address all over again (see the following two screenshots):

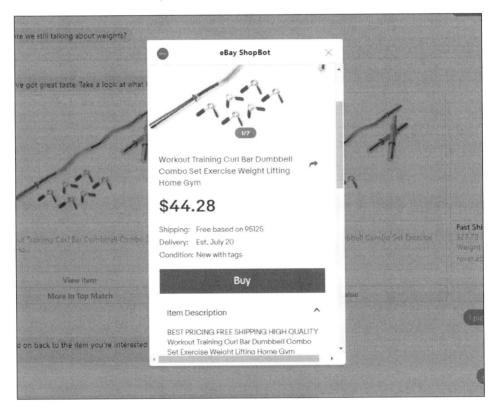

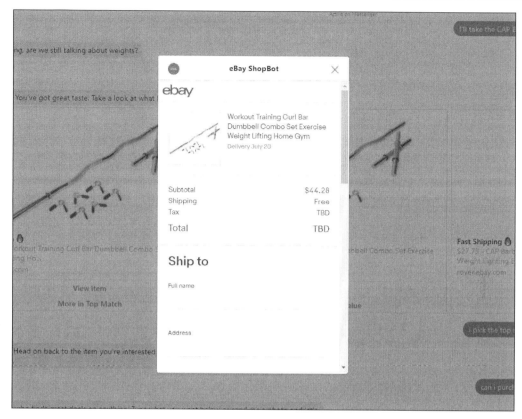

Figure 14 and 15: Sometimes a web view is required to complete secure processes. For an optimal result, the screen width should be taken into consideration.

Summary

The travel and e-commerce industries are both fascinating use cases for any digital evolution. Unlike many other industries, digital solutions have managed to replace whole functions and even professions, or at least minimized them. It is therefore interesting to see how these two industries, which are always pioneers in the market, are reacting to automatic conversational solutions, and how they deal with the limitations and challenges that these solutions bring with them.

For a long while, chatbots' added value wasn't clear to many industries, but as technology evolves, the use cases are revealing themselves slowly. It is clear to see that the market is approaching these solutions with much caution, however, some of the leading brands are already experimenting with some more advanced capabilities.

I chose KAYAK and eBay for this chapter's examples, since they are far more advanced in the market with their voicebots and chatbots implementation. There is a lot we can learn from the smooth experience these bots provide, as well as their thought-out interactions. Clearly, there is always room for improvement, but looking at the evolution of these solutions over time, those two examples can definitely become a good standard to follow.

Last but not least, both companies are dealing with the complexity of data discovery with chatbots and voicebots. While in the KAYAK example, this was clearer on the Alexa example, both brands have given a lot of thought to the data discovery experience and how it can be solved.

To reach good results for data discovery, today's search engines will have to be able to provide much more accurate results and show that they really understand the user's needs.

In the next chapter, we will design a conversational application together and walk through all the stages that we have outlined in this book.

References

- Mobile shopping surpass desktop - `https://techcrunch.com/2017/11/02/mobile-holiday-shopping-visits-in-u-s-will-surpass-desktop-for-first-time/`.

- eBay ShopBot: `https://www.messenger.com/t/ebayshopbot`

- KAYAK FB bot: `https://www.messenger.com/t/kayak`

- KAYAK on Amazon Alexa: `https://www.amazon.com/gp/product/B00P03D4D2/ref=mas_pm_kayak` or go to `alexa.amazon.com` and then search for "KAYAK"

- Ivy: `https://chatbotsmagazine.com/ivy-is-a-a-24-hour-virtual-concierge-service-that-smooths-the-stay-of-guests-at-hotels-raj-singh-12ceacd5cd7b`

- Gooster: `https://gooster.net/`

~ 10 ~

CONVERSATIONAL DESIGN PROJECT – A STEP-BY-STEP GUIDE

In the previous nine chapters, we have discussed all there is to know about conversational applications. We have talked about the technical aspects and the psychological aspects, and given some examples of what we should do and what we shouldn't do when building a conversational solution.

Indeed, there is so much that needs to be taken into consideration that it might seem overwhelming. So how do we take all those recommendations and implement them? Where do we begin?

This chapter is your hands-on guide for designing conversational applications. We will outline the steps we need to follow to build conversational applications and, maybe even more importantly, how to maintain them and keep them relevant as they evolve.

We will use all the concepts that we have discussed in this book and see how we can implement them in practice.

For the purpose of this guide, I've chosen to build a banking conversational bot, as it combines simple and complex requirements. As already outlined in the book, since the guiding concepts for building successful conversational applications are universal, you can use this guide for any other vertical as well.

Defining the stakeholders

This, of course, may change from one organization to another, but, in general, a successful bot is the result of the joint efforts of:

1. Business and marketing – setting the goals
2. IT and R&D – technical implementation
3. UI/UX and creative – design implementation

Each department has its functionality and an impact on the success of the bot. In many cases, some of these stakeholders are overlooked and the work is left just for the technical team. However, remember, building a conversational solution is not only a technical task – it's a business, marketing, UI, UX, and creative task. In some cases, the initiative will come from the business/marketing side and in some cases from the R&D/ IT teams.

You can use the following chart as a tool to fill in the names of the relevant people for your project. In some cases, you might need to use the help of an external resource, if you don't have some of these functions in your organization.

This group of people will continue to be involved in the maintenance and growth of the conversational solution after deployment. We will refer to that later in this chapter.

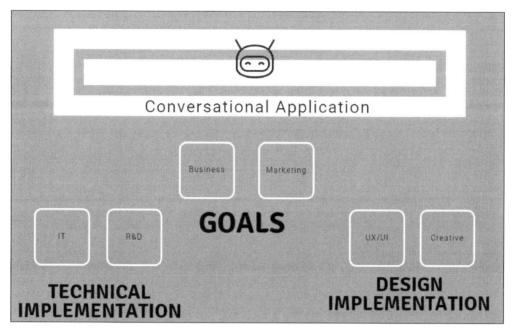

Figure 1: Building a group: defining and deciding on the stakeholders

Including all the relevant stakeholders is important to make sure that all aspects of the bot are covered and it also creates a committed group of people who share and understand the project and contribute to it all along. Some of the tasks will require the intervention of more than one group or person. Putting this list of people together in advance will contribute to the success of the bot in the setup and maintenance phase.

For the purpose of our demo banking bot, let's assume that the initiative came from the marketing team. In this case, I will include a representative from R&D and IT, as well as from the UI/UX team. We don't have a creative team, so I will search for external relevant candidates to include.

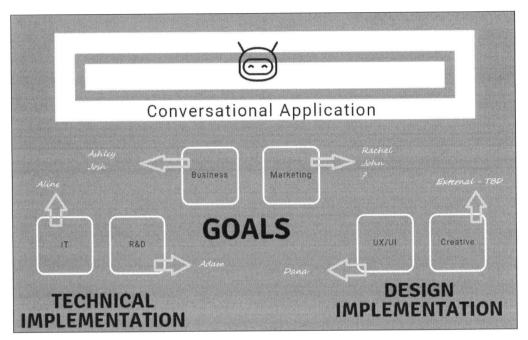

Figure 2: Build your group: add your partners to the project

Defining the goals

This stage is a building block of every conversational solution. We have discussed throughout the book that a bot doesn't have its own essence and that it must serve a specific need, or multiple ones. Only after we define the goals can we dive into building functionality, design, experience, and more.

The task of defining the goal of the bot will usually be the responsibility of the business and marketing team. When defining the goals, we should ask and provide answers to the following:

♦ What is the bot's overall goal?

♦ Why is this the goal?

♦ What are the current solutions we use? What do they lack?

♦ What would the bot do better?

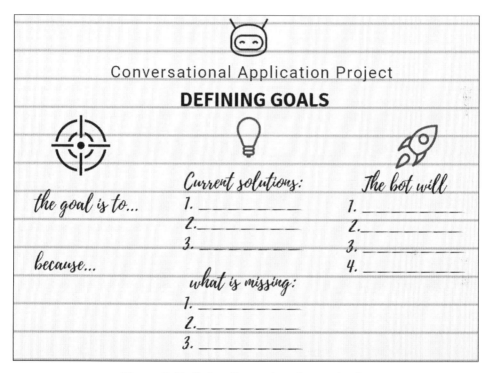

Conversational Application Project

DEFINING GOALS

the goal is to...

because...

Current solutions:
1. _____
2. _____
3. _____

what is missing:
1. _____
2. _____
3. _____

The bot will
1. _____
2. _____
3. _____
4. _____

Figure 3: Defining the goals: what and why

Going back to our example, we can answer these questions as follows:

♦ The goal of the bot is to provide conversational self-service channels for general and account-related actions, as well as offering sales-related support

- To be able to provide our clients with good service at scale and to reduce the organization's operational costs
- Today we offer online banking on desktop and mobile, phone banking, and an IVR call center
- The bot will:
  - Increase accessibility by providing additional endpoints to interact with on new and existing solutions
  - Reduce 50% of call center requests and costs by handling these automatically
  - Increase sales leads by 25%
  - Present the company as innovative

Who does our bot address?

By understanding who will use our bot, we will later be able to define its persona accordingly and even the design (chat and voice) that we will use to build our conversational solution.

When analyzing our target group, we should take into consideration a variety of parameters:

- Age
- Gender
- Function: employee/customer-facing
- Vertical (if relevant)
- Geography
- Language

These six parameters will usually have subcategories and sub-parameters, and they might not always have one strict option. A bot can also address people in multiple languages. Knowing this in advance will help us to be prepared on the design and the technical side, as we move along. We will deep dive into our target groups once we start to build our bot's persona.

In our banking example, we decided to focus on the bank's customers. The age group will be 25-45, male and female. We will support one language, English, with the goal of expanding to Spanish and German.

Where and how – choosing devices

Next we need to define the devices and channels we would like our bot to be available on: should it be on voice or chat? Should it run on a third-party platform or on our own digital real estate?

We have defined some of the leading devices and channels throughout this book and have emphasized their advantages and disadvantages. As a true believer in cross-channel support, I believe that when we are building a conversational solution, it should (eventually) become available on multiple devices and channels, creating a continuous experience across multiple mediums.

With that being said, for some verticals and industries, text solutions will make more sense, whereas in others, voice-enabled ones will have more success. This is a question you should be addressing as you build your project's strategy and as you evaluate and adjust it. New devices and mediums appear pretty often, so you might find yourself adding additional support as you go.

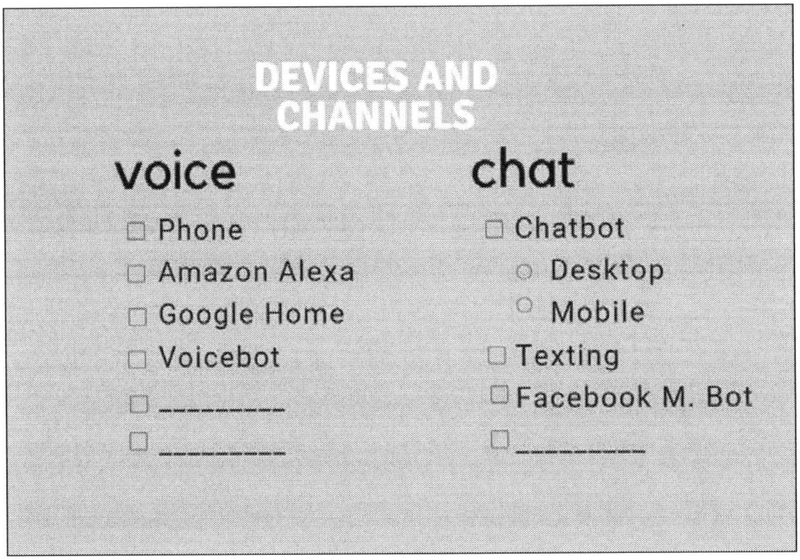

Figure 4: Chat, voice, or both – what channels will serve your goals?

Going back to our banking example, and paying attention to the goals and the target market, our group has made the decision to:

♦ Build a cross-channel experience that will include both voice and chat, both on new mediums, such as texting, but also on existing ones, such as adding a chatbot to the website

♦ Include automation of the most common and repetitive use cases of the call centers over the phone

♦ Offer solutions on Amazon Alexa and Google Home to present the organization as innovative.

Our conversational application's persona

In *Chapter 7*, *Building Personalities – Your Bot Can Be a Better Human*, we discussed the importance of a bot's persona and how it serves us and our clients. Now that we know who our target market is, and where our conversational application will be available on chat and voice, we can focus more on the bot's persona.

The Austin Beer persona, Kit, invited us to focus on:

- The bot's name
- Its goal, which we have already identified
- What it does – already identified broadly
- What it thinks
- How it feels

We also added how it looks and sounds and what language it uses. Let's see how this works in our example: we work for bank "ABC", so we will call our bot the "ABC Virtual Assistant."

We believe that people will find it easier to talk to the face of a human when they interact. Since the clear majority of our employees are women, we will give the bot the face of a lady. With this in mind, we will also choose a woman's voice for our voicebot, as well as our Alexa and Google Home applications.

We will have the same persona on all of our channels.

Being a bank's bot, we will also make sure that we keep the interaction's language formal and polite.

Here she is:

Figure 5: Our banking bot persona: "Hi, I'm ABC's Personal Assistant"

Functionality and use cases

Defining and implementing the functions of the conversational application is probably the biggest and longest part of the setup process, and also of the maintenance process. Identifying what your bot actually does includes:

♦ Defining the use cases based on the goals – business/ marketing

♦ Creating the relevant conversational flows – business/ marketing/UX

♦ Building the business logic – IT/R&D

♦ Providing samples – business/marketing/creative

♦ Providing answers – business/creative

♦ Connecting to APIs – IT/ R&D

Building the functionality of our bot requires the intervention of all stakeholder groups. The business group will need to provide the use cases that the bot will cover. This will be based on our previous analysis, where we have identified what the bot's goals are and what it should do better than current solutions.

The conversational flow will be defined by the business/marketing/creative and UX groups. Building a conversational flow means framing the potential discussions that our target group will hold with our bot. This means taking our use cases and breaking them down into specific questions.

To support our NLU engines, we will need to provide similar sentences for each question. As you may recall, it is recommended to start with at least 15 samples. The more you can provide, the better your bot will be able to respond to the user's questions. Compiling the samples requires the help of creative people. They should come up with enough variations of a specific question.

Creative people are also involved when we provide the answers. On top of connecting our systems with the relevant APIs, which helps us to extract the relevant data based on the user's request, we need to make sure that the bot replies with a full conversational sentence and doesn't just spit out the information.

Answers can differ from one device to another, as well as between different channels. When using a textual solution, we can use emojis to express certain feelings, however, we can't do that when using voice. On the other hand, we can use an MP3 file to sing "happy birthday" to the user when we use a voice-enabled solution, which we can't do using text.

Creating a holistic experience between different channels will result in success. Looking at our example, when the user asks a Google Home device for the nearest ATM location, we will provide the answer using voice and refer the user to the corresponding app for directions, using Google Maps. The Alexa cart doesn't support maps, so we can offer to text the user the address and combine another method of interaction to complete the first one more successfully.

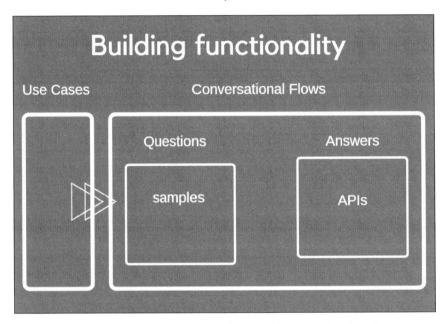

Figure 6: The bot's business logic and interaction levels

Let's see how this will work in our banking example. To define the use cases, the business and marketing teams have agreed on four use case categories and, within each use case, the specific topics (that we previously defined as intents):

1. General questions: opening hours, branch locations, and routing number

2. Account-related questions: balance, transactions, and insights

3. Actionable requests: transfer money or pay bill

4. Sales support use cases: loan rates and loan applications

For each of the preceding intents, the business and marketing teams will come up with two-to-three question samples. The creative team will expand the options accordingly.

Let's take the example of opening hours. The business/marketing teams have come up with the obvious question:

What are your opening hours?

The creative team will take this sentence and create variations, which are what we call samples or utterances. It could be by simply using synonyms or by totally rephrasing the request:

When are you open?

Are you open on Fridays?

When can I come to your offices?

Since it is very difficult to think of all the different ways people may ask for something, using a tool to help you monitor that can be very helpful.

Now, it's time to connect the questions to the answers. The R&D or the IT teams will assist by connecting the APIs of the systems to each question/request. The business/marketing team will formulate and draft the response, and the creative team will provide additional variations to avoid a monotonous experience and to adapt to the relevant channels:

We are open every weekday between <opening hours APIs>.

You are welcome to visit us Monday to Friday between <opening hours APIs>.

Our opening hours are <opening hours APIs> on weekdays.

Development and testing

The development of our conversational application is where R&D takes on the most important role. Whether building solutions from scratch or using some of the available solutions and toolkits, R&D will be responsible for translating our conversations into code, delivering the business logic across all channels and devices.

To be able to build the solution, R&D, based on the preceding work, will build a technical flow, which will take into consideration multiple scenarios and requirements. Those flow charts, or for voice solutions, **Voice User Interfaces** (**VUI**), are based on specific building blocks that represent certain functionalities.

You can use Google Drawings for that or any of the available solutions on the market. The following flowchart is an example of a request loan rate conversational flow, which takes into consideration the need for authentication.

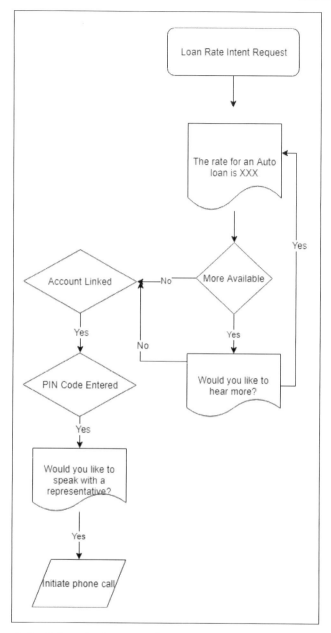

Figure 7: Building the business logic: preparing the conversational
flow for R&D to program

The preceding conversational flow chart will also assist as we test our bot. Testing is extremely important and we need to make sure that we cover the use cases we planned for in the broadest way. After the initial project group has tested the solution, it is recommended to create a closed "user group" of colleagues, or even some customers, who will be given access to the solution to test it from various devices and provide feedback. This process is very similar to any other digital **Software Development Life Cycles** (**SDLC**) that we are familiar with.

Deployment, maintenance, and analytics

After testing our bot and deploying it on the relevant devices and channels, we come to the important part of maintenance. We have mentioned over and over that building a conversational solution is not a one-time project and that there will be a constant need to modify, change, enhance, and improve as we bring our bot into contact with the users.

All stakeholders must continue to play an active part in the maintenance process. Marketing and business teams are needed, since some of the improvements will include adding more use cases. UI and UX designers will be required, in case of linguistic changes to new and current use cases or to revise the bot's persona. In all use cases, R&D will be required to implement those modifications.

Learning our clients' behavior will help us to improve our conversational solutions. Only when we see how people react to our bot *in numbers* can we conclude whether our bot is fulfilling its goals.

Analytics will provide insights into an array of metrics, including the number of messages and sessions, the number of messages per user, the number of users over time, the devices and channels used, and the number of failed conversations. All of those figures will help us to rate how successful our conversational solution is.

After learning from our analytics about the basic behavior of our clients with our bot, we can add A/B testing measurements to our conversational solutions to dig deeper into understanding which paths work better and which maximize our clients' experience. A/B testing can run on the same channel/device or different channels. It can alternate between two different flows for the same intent even just between different types of responses to the same request. The more we look into our customers' behavior, the better our bot will become.

In our use case, we will make sure that the number of calls to our call centers is decreasing and that our customer satisfaction rate has increased.

Maintenance will also include adding support to more conversational devices and channels. In our case, we started with a few chat and voice devices, and we can now expand to support more endpoints.

Figure 8 (appendix): "Conversational Application Design Checklist"

Summary

In this chapter, we took all that we have learned in the book and created a practical project. We went through the required steps and made sure we paid attention to all of the design principals we discussed in the book.

Following a methodology can help with achieving successful results. I've added a project list as an appendix (figure 8), which you can use for each conversational project you start. You can use it as it is or customize it for your own unique needs. Even if you knowingly decide to skip one or two steps, the list can still help you as you continue to revise and improve your conversational bots.

While we have discussed most of the steps in the book, one important point that I mentioned briefly, but that is extremely important when you start your conversational project, is to make sure that all of the relevant stakeholders are involved in the process from as early as possible.

It goes without saying that a conversational solution without pre-defined goals cannot succeed. Those goals can change along the way, but if we can't identify the goals in advance, we won't be able to build our bot correctly.

With this in mind, of course, the use cases and conversational flows are of utmost importance, as well as the broad "dictionary" of sample sentences and unique responses that come along with it. Don't build your bot to fail – build it for success. Help it to deal with real users in the real world.

Lastly, test your bot, modify it, expand it, clarify it, test it again, and analyze it repeatedly. Your conversational solution, like every other successful digital asset, needs attention to prove its effectiveness.

~ 11 ~

SUMMARY

Writing this book was an exciting and uplifting experience for me. For the past two years, my life has revolved around conversational experiences on voice and chat, and being able to share this information with more readers and conversational revolutionists feels like a true blessing.

While writing this book, a lot has changed in this extremely fast-growing and dynamic market. New devices and new capabilities have been introduced, and I literally needed to rewrite some parts of the book due to newly introduced features and capabilities from Google. It might be that, in a few months from now, some of the book's insights and predictions will become void, as technology and expertise continue to grow and advance.

I started the book with the declaration that "conversational user interface is changing the way that we interact" and I do believe that this is the main message of my book. We are witnessing a paradigm shift in communication, which we are familiar with from the science fiction movies we all grew up on. Businesses that fail to adapt will not be able to continue communicating with their clients as they are expected to, both on the support and the sales side.

In this summary chapter, I want to shortly recap what has been discussed throughout this book and give some insights into the future of conversational design.

Conversational interfaces – how did it all start and where do we stand today?

We started by talking about where it all began. Understanding the progress of human-machine interfaces helps us to understand the evolution from textual interfaces to graphical interfaces, and all the way to conversational UI, and can assist in making assumptions and predictions for future changes.

We took a deeper dive into the conversational stack, understanding the different technologies that support conversational UI today as it evolves. We are lucky to be at a phase in this journey where many of the fundamental layers of this stack are solid and stable, and this allows us to build and grow unique and sophisticated conversational applications that we couldn't have dreamed of only a few years back. This includes voice-recognition and text-to-speech capabilities, and even more important are NLU abilities, which have completely changed the game and allowed us to start experimenting with contextual conversation with explicit and implicit structures.

With that being said, and with all of our accomplishments over the past few years, we still face many challenges with conversational applications and, more specifically, their ability to mimic and replace traditionally human-led services.

While we have advanced tremendously with NLU capabilities, we still face the problem that NLU is an AI-hard problem, meaning that even with the help of AI we are struggling to provide high-quality solutions. Unexpected circumstances, in the form of endless configurations of words and sentences, in an endless number of languages and dialects, are the main cause of that. Many companies address this problem, and when we look into the future, we should expect to see huge progress in NLU capabilities. Conversational solutions will not be able to progress and prevail without that.

On the UX side, the transition from GUI to CUI and, even more specifically, VUX still exposes many challenges in the user's behavior and expectations, and the ability of businesses to communicate over these short-focused channels, which are in some cases are also screenless. I have shown in the book that, in some cases, the need to overcome the challenges surrounding NLU and content discovery has led to the development of limited conversational solutions, which have forced web experience onto chatbot channels, and provided no efficiency or added value for the users.

The security and privacy challenges, which companies and users are still struggling with, are another hurdle in the way of helping conversational solutions to prevail. As I was writing the book, the Facebook data privacy scandal erupted, raising more concerns and uncertainty around this topic.

This is not to say that chatbots and voice-enabled conversations are doomed, however, business and platform providers will have to come up with a more compelling approach. Users are now much more cautious and aware of the risks of sharing their personal data, especially on devices and channels from third-party providers, such as Amazon Alexa, Google Home and, of course, FB Messenger. This might be the reason that many financial institutions have chosen to start building their conversational applications as proprietary (available via web/app/texting), before they make them available on third-party solutions.

As this space continues to evolve, I predict that data privacy and data ownership issues will have to be handled with extra care, both by businesses and providers. This might also be grounds for the rise of new platforms that promise data privacy to companies and their users, as we see today in the health industry.

Two other challenges we addressed in this book, as we explored conversational solutions in the travel and e-commerce industries, are:

♦ The need to compete with existing solutions that simply work very well

♦ The discovery challenge

While the first challenge emphasizes the need to build conversational UI that provides real value, and improves efficiency and costs (which is common when transitioning from one solution to another), the second challenge touches upon an acute problem: defining a new discovery model (the industry has started to address this lately) and we will have to give that a whole lot of thought as we progress.

Last, but not least, conversational UI is still limited because users are still skeptical of it. We had great expectations from chatbots, but today, aware of the limitations, businesses and users stick to simplicity and tend to not challenge it too much. As technology evolves and more companies start challenging the limitations of conversational UI, we will see the rise of more complex and advanced solutions, which will really make our life more efficient and our communications more focused.

At the end, as I've already stated in the book, creating a supercomputer that "knows everything" is more in reach than creating a super-knowledgeable person. Technology, whether in the form of advanced AI, **machine learning (ML)**, or **deep learning (DL)** methodologies, will solve most of those challenges. I predict that human skepticism will vanish alongside this.

Why do we even need conversational solutions? What do they bring to the table?

When asked about the future of chatbots and voicebots, I always answer that conversational solutions and, more specifically, voice-enabled communication, will replace all our interactions with computers. Why? It is because conversational solutions are here to make our lives easier and better, and humankind has always looked for ways to improve communication and their quality of life.

Intelligent assistants, chatbots, and voice-enabled devices are here to provide a natural and intuitive human-machine interaction to serve human needs. They increase efficiency and are cost-effective, but - and this is a big but - only if and when they are built and implemented correctly.

A few chapters in the book were dedicated to tips and ideas on how to build a successful conversational UI for both chat and voice applications. We actually started by identifying what not to do, since those mistakes are very common, and to some extent they are a response to some of today's technology barriers.

Conversational solutions are expected to mimic natural human conversation. More simply said, we use a natural voice/ text communication method to express what we want, without being required to interact with another person. In today's world, where we are used to achieving things fast and furiously, this is a win-win situation for businesses – saving on costs – and for the end users – who save on time.

Replacing human interaction, however, is not as simple as we would like it to be. That's why, as we have shown, many chatbots end up mimicking a web or an app experience, which offers the exact opposite of a concise and focused interaction. Providing endless unclassified data doesn't make the bot better – on the contrary, it makes it impractical. However, there is a catch here: one should avoid a situation where too little information is provided. On the path of offering a concise interaction, we have to keep the balance between too much and too little, and listen to our users, and their requirements and expectations.

How to build great conversational applications

While it's easy to say what not to do, I tried to include as many positive examples as possible in the book, focusing also on what we should do when we build our conversational applications and continue to maintain them. *Chapter 3*, *Building a Killer Conversational App*. described in more detail what is needed to build a "killer app," both from a technical point of view and from a UX one.

As mentioned previously, conversational UI is an extremely new field in computing and it is also extremely dynamic. Therefore, some things that weren't available just a few months back are now an integral part of each solution (for example, the option to choose between different voices, the ability to build contextual interactions, and coming back to a user if the bot has learned a new function or information on Amazon Alexa). You have to make sure to keep yourself informed and aware of those changes and progress, if you want to achieve the best results for you and your users.

While building our "killer app," we discussed the fact that we want our users to succeed at interacting with our bot and how we can help them to get there, sometimes by simply being honest with them and letting them know they are talking to an automated solution and not a real human agent. We discussed the need to think big and learn from the "forefathers" of conversational UI, mainly the search engine, to provide a good and open communication experience. We also discussed the known challenge of devices' fragmentation and diversity, and how we should address this by providing a multi-channel experience across all (or most) platforms and devices.

Development: technical and non-technical expertise

Conversational UI opens many opportunities up to non-technical professionals. Voice and chat designers, creatives, data scientists, and persona builders are all responsible for bringing life to a machine-built bot. As a non-developer myself, I know this is a thrilling and rewarding experience.

However, building a bot still requires figuring out the technicalities behind that. I devoted three chapters to the procedures behind building conversational applications for Amazon Alexa, Google Home, and FB Messenger. Even though I deal with this on a daily basis, I still needed the help of some of my colleagues to jump over some fences.

While those platforms do make the effort to offer some tools for non-developers, the capabilities offered by them are very simple and minimal. Some third-party companies try to fill the gap, however, building a complex UX for a bot, with advanced AI capabilities, still requires the cooperation of developers.

That being said, just like building websites, I predict that in the future more capabilities will become available for non-developers to build conversational solutions. As industry leaders, those companies will play a great role in shaping the growth of conversational UI, and making it easier to build is an important part of that. In the meanwhile, close cooperation between developers and non-developers is required to build a successful conversational application. All relevant stakeholders are needed for the process, both in the setup and the maintenance phases.

It is worth emphasizing that since conversational UI is replacing human interactions, the role of persona designers, as well as linguistic creative teams, is extremely important, and they contribute both to the character and the emotional intelligence of the bot. Being able to talk in the user's language, as well as to identify and detect emotional states, helps the bot to navigate the conversation down a more successful path. This is part of what was discussed in the book about a bot's "humanization" process.

Vertical-specific or a mega bot?

Where will the future take us when it comes to the bot's capabilities? Will we continue to focus on vertical-specific conversational UIs, as we have seen in our examples of banks, travel, and e-commerce bots, or will we turn to the know-all intelligent assistants, that can do everything? Will we be able to create that "mega brain" that will be able to differentiate between use cases from various aspects of life and provide us with a one-stop shop for all our needs?

As I stated in the last two chapters, I believe we will gradually move from the domain-specific to the "mega brain" in the next decade. The concept of personal assistants, such as Siri and Alexa, will expand to allow cross-application interactions and recommendations. This highly complicated task requires lots and lots of data to be able to deal with our AI-hard obstacle, but it will probably be achieved as those solutions continue to evolve.

It also seems, that, in order to get to that last point, we must go through the vertical-specific path. We saw how financial institutions, travel, and e-commerce companies build a whole new expertise into conversational applications, and how they continue to evolve over time, based on their continuous learnings and understandings. Figuring out all the possible use cases is a tough task that requires lots of knowledge and data, however, once this process is completed (and I believe this is a long process, due to the high number of unexpected circumstances), we will be able to start passing information between different verticals and bring them all under one roof.

Summary

Building cognitive conversational UI is still a very new and dynamic area. This book aimed to provide some insights, ideas, and a methodology to follow when accomplishing this thrilling task.

Looking to the future, we understand that technical progress is required to build the real *HAL 9000* and this is indeed where technology innovations are heading. However, it was crucial for me to stress the importance of the non-technical aspects of building a conversational solution, and the human-related (and non-technical) obstacles that we see today and that will have to change in the future.

While the book offers a hands-on guidance for the world of conversational UI, it also seeks to stretch your thinking, so that you visualize conversational solutions in the future and what your role will be in shaping that future. If you are reading this book, you obviously believe in the future of conversational design and the fact that the journey has started, and there's no going back. I hope you have found this book supportive and accommodating, and that it has helped you to take your first steps into the conversational world.

OTHER BOOK YOU MAY ENJOY

If you enjoyed this book, you may be interested in this book by Packt:

Hands-On Chatbots and Conversational UI Development

Srini Janarthanam

ISBN: 978-1-78829-466-9

- Design the flow of conversation between the user and the chatbot
- Create Task model chatbots for implementing tasks such as ordering food
- Get new toolkits and services in the chatbot ecosystem
- Integrate third-party information APIs to build interesting chatbots
- Find out how to deploy chatbots on messaging platforms
- Build a chatbot using MS Bot Framework
- See how to tweet, listen to tweets, and respond using a chatbot on Twitter
- Publish chatbots on Google Assistant and Amazon Alexa

Leave a review - let other readers know what you think

Please share your thoughts on this book with others by leaving a review on the site that you bought it from. If you purchased the book from Amazon, please leave us an honest review on this book's Amazon page. This is vital so that other potential readers can see and use your unbiased opinion to make purchasing decisions, we can understand what our customers think about our products, and our authors can see your feedback on the title that they have worked with Packt to create. It will only take a few minutes of your time, but is valuable to other potential customers, our authors, and Packt. Thank you!

Index

Printed in Great Britain
by Amazon

46728186R00169